A Richer Dust

A RICHER DUST

Colin Gordon

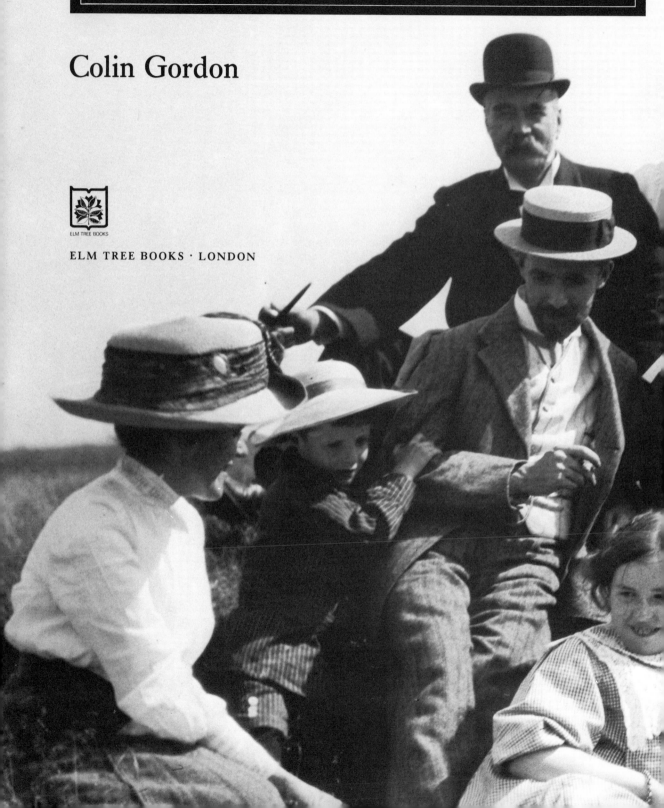

ELM TREE BOOKS · LONDON

Echoes from an Edwardian Album

For Christine

British Library Cataloguing in Publication Data

Gordon, Colin
  A richer dust.
  1. Great Britain—Social life and customs—
  19th century 2. Great Britain—Social life and
  customs—20th century
  I. Title
  941.081   DA533

  ISBN 0-241-89934-6

First published in Great Britain 1978
by Elm Tree Books/Hamish Hamilton Ltd
90 Great Russell Street, London WC1B 3PT

Designed by Lawrence Edwards

© 1978 by Colin Gordon

Filmset and printed in Great Britain by
BAS Printers Limited, Over Wallop, Hampshire

Contents

Acknowledgements

I CANNOT REMEMBER any one moment when this book was conceived; rather it crept upon me and I found myself the foster parent. Most of the work described in the book was done with no eye to publication. Neither the story nor the photographs are fully mine, though I hope I have nurtured them. I thank those whose interest and encouragement first made a book possible, especially Mr George Perry of *The Sunday Times* and Mr Bill Greaves of B.B.C. North.

The Atkinson family and their friends have allowed me to trespass freely and have all shared their memories with me. It will become obvious that one family trait is unbounded hospitality. For that I am very grateful. Mr Peter Bennett of Trinity and All Saints Colleges, Horsforth, near Leeds, also helped me trace some of the Atkinson family and friends. His initiative and tact lie behind some of the memories in the latter part of the book.

My research—though 'research' is too inhuman a word for the less formal side—was done during school holidays, at weekends and in the hours between marking piles of exercise books. To write, however, I needed an uninterrupted span. I thank the headmaster and governors of Queen Elizabeth Grammar School, Wakefield, for allowing me the time, and the warden and fellows of Merton College, Oxford, for providing a setting so welcoming, stimulating and beautiful. The squirrels in Christchurch meadow have played their part: to write in a room with such a view was the final stroke of good fortune which makes the whole project a classic definition of 'serendipity'.

I have been asked several times about the title of this book. It comes from the most famous of Rupert Brooke's five war sonnets, 'The Soldier', written at the end of 1914:

. . . There shall be
In that rich earth a richer dust concealed.

Finally, I am grateful to Mr and Mrs R. E. Ellis of Berkhamstead for permission to reproduce five photographs by Mr H. M. Hastings; to the Literary Executors of Mrs A. Wynick and Chatto and Windus for permission to quote from the poem, 'August, 1914', from Isaac Rosenberg's *Collected Poems*; and to Laurie Lee and The Hogarth Press for permission to use a phrase from *Cider With Rosie*.

1

'ATKINSON, HUBY'

I HAVE NEVER been a passionate collector of things. As a boy I had the obligatory stamp album but the delights of its empty pages soon staled. I was never excited by train numbers; nor did I fill my bedroom with fossils or match-box labels. However, I did not entirely escape the mania of searching for trivia. I date my infection from the time I moved into an unfurnished flat as a schoolteacher in Bradford, Yorkshire, in the late 1960s. Previously, furniture in my rooms had been inescapably there, not to my taste but not a matter of choice. Now, with a flat to furnish, I decided to buy what I liked, not necessarily what I needed.

I bought a grandfather clock first. It stood in otherwise empty rooms, and I slept, or failed to sleep, on the floor, since beds came low on my list of priorities. There was, however, satisfaction to be gained from identifying with others who made unconventional choices, like the prince in a story by 'Saki' who grew pigs instead of flowers in his garden.

Bradford at that time still had its junk shops—not always shops—more often condemned properties bulging with cast-offs. They spilled their stuff out across the pavement and road. There was no swank about these places; they sold what they advertised— junk—and valued it at no more. 'Antiques' belonged to a much more pretentious circuit. However, if you browsed round the junk shops long enough, you might find something invaluable among the un- valued. Slowly I filled the empty spaces in my flat and developed what I can only call a penchant for clocks and chairs.

The real junk shops, however, were rapidly closing, victims partly of urban clearance orders and their own dilapidation. Even more devastating in its effect on the junk shops was the new breed of dealers in junk—the 'fleamarket' men. Like most really successful entrepreneurs, they conceived of a scheme of primitive simplicity. They, the bigger

fleas, hire a large hall for the day and sell stalls to the smaller fleas who sell their goods ... *ad infinitum.* These fleamarkets attract both antiques and junk and, rubbing shoulders, they grow alike. Nowadays we have to pay as much for junk as we once paid for rare pieces.

In this way fleamarkets have made the 'big find' a vain hope. Even the most humble of dealers knows his 'nickle-plated' from his 'silver'. He will not let gold run through his fingers; he is more likely to try and pass off all that glisters. The only true junk stalls left are in the darker corners of open street markets. Here the part-timers still offer unconsidered trifles for pence rather than pounds.

In 1972 I moved to a new teaching post in Wakefield and, during routine Saturday shopping, I made it a habit to glance at the market junk stalls, not exactly in hope but more in surprise at what was offered for sale. Could anyone be interested in second-hand plumbing, scratched long-playing records or obsolete school books? One stall in particular was the perfect answer to sceptics. Here everything was auctioned, from teaspoons to trou- sers, and the dozens who clustered round, caught up in the bidding, actually vied for what no one could want.

One Saturday in August 1975, I set off for the market in search of cheap vegetables and fruit. On one of the junk stalls, flanked by mountains of old clothes, were scattered a score or more of small boxes. Printed on some of them were chemical names which meant as much to me as the doings of alchemists—pyrogallic acid, sulphite of soda, am- monium bromide and the like. Intrigued, I opened one box and found it full of glass photographic negatives, the first one in a paper sachet and titled, 'Grasmere Lake, Easter Monday, 1897' (Plate 91). Queen Victoria's Diamond Jubliee year was distant enough to excite my interest. This was also the first time I had ever seen photographic negatives of any age offered for sale.

That in itself is strange: most middle-class families since the turn of the century have owned more photographs than books but, whereas books are the roughage of the junk dealer's diet, negatives are a very rare dish. What happens to them? Are negatives simply too plain even for those ready to label everything 'antique'? Photographs, however, link us more immediately with people of the past than most of what we value; they are more truly personal. Furniture and domestic trappings may have been slaves to many; but to own a man's negatives is more of a privilege and, perhaps, even a trespass.

Something of this sense of pocketing another man's life made me want to buy the negatives. I knew that too much interest would double the price but I was as yet no more than curious. The price was seven pounds. Without the slightest idea of the negatives' market value and without the cheek to be a good haggler, I still thought that seven pounds was too much. So I offered five: there might not have been anything of real interest in the boxes. Lamenting his minimal profit, the stall-holder gave way and I lost the most important five-pound note I had ever spent.

Five pounds was actually enough to make me feel rash at the time. The stall-holder was, I think, happy to be relieved of the sheer weight of several hundred pieces of glass. Had I not bought them, they might have been reduced to splinters at the day's end. It was a hard enough job for me to get them home intact.

As I struggled half a mile to my car on a hot Saturday morning with a large cardboard box full of glass, shedding a few stray pieces and resting every few yards, I was impressed in a physical way by what I had taken on. Unlike my previous whimsical buys, this one would not justify its cost by gracing the sitting-room after routine cleaning. If there were any surprises or secrets, they would not be given up easily. In the first place, while I could develop and print the kind of photographs I might take on holiday or at weekends, I had no equipment to handle glass negatives larger than postcards; I knew nothing about the cameras of my great-grandparents' time; and I had no idea whose negatives I had bought.

What, exactly, had I bought? In all, there were about thirty boxes containing over 650 negatives in two sizes which I later learned to call half-plate ($6\frac{1}{2}$ × $4\frac{3}{4}$ inches) and quarter-plate ($4\frac{1}{4}$ × $3\frac{1}{4}$ inches). The larger negatives were in boxes of a dozen, clearly the boxes in which they had been bought, manufactured by Elliott and Fry at Barnet, Herts. Happily, the captions and some of the dates (the earliest 1887) were written on the boxes—although the names often failed tantalisingly to correspond to the contents. Most of the smaller negatives were also in boxes according to subject or occasion, such as 'Polly' (Plates 1 and 2), 'Miscellaneous Boats' (Plates 3 and 4) or 'Mixed Groups' (Plates 5–7).

I was surprised not to find those glassy-eyed portraits which fill the pages of ornate, old family albums. These pictures, I suspected were more truly amateur—a private and incidental record of frozen moments. Even an uninformed eye, however, could see that in addition to these family snapshots proudly recording the growth of children and the accidental pleasures of holidays and outings (Plates 8–10), there were many pictures more aptly called 'studies': figures posed in landscapes or caught in lanes (Plates 11 and 12), recognisable beauty spots in Yorkshire (Plates 13–15) and so on. Nevertheless, the appearance of the same people on so many of the photographs made it a fair guess that they were the work of a single amateur. But who?

I searched through the boxes and scraps of paper wrapped around the negatives and found just one clue. There was an invoice from a photographic shop in Harrogate made out to a customer. He was clearly well known at the shop because his name and address were abbreviated and reduced almost to cipher: 'Atkinson, Huby'. These two words hardly said much but they were at least a start and I was excited at the idea of adding to them.

Looking back, I cannot fully explain my eagerness. I was at least old enough to feel nostalgia and not be embarrassed by it. As a result, I shared the universal fascination for the apparently secure world before the First World War. My impressions of it, however, were only stereotypes lit by sunshine. Television had shown me elegant ladies in outrageous hats under parasols taking tea on a green and pleasant lawn to airs from a regimental band. Television had also taught me that the gap between this world and its servants could be measured in vowel sounds and flights of stairs. I think, however, the really haunting attraction of this two-storey world lay in its being so palpably different yet not impossibly distant. Most of us have relatives with memories of that time and can mourn the loss of its illusory sense of security. In exchanging Edwardian complacency for the freedom to doubt and to question, we secretly feel we have a bad bargain:

The gold, the honey gone—
Left is the hard and the cold.[1]

In cultural terms, then, the turn of the century has acquired the status of classical golden age or paradise before the fall. My boxes of negatives were a tangible link with that world and I decided to unearth what I could of the photographer and his family.

The decision to revive the dead, however, was not entirely mine to make. I was supposed to be setting off the following week for a holiday in Cornwall with a friend, who knew nothing as yet of the negatives and might not agree that the mystery of 'Atkinson, Huby' justified giving up a holiday in the south. However, I carefully marshalled the arguments against going to Cornwall: uncertain weather, certain traffic jams and the like. Fortunately, when Christine saw some of the pictures, she shared my enthusiasm. So we cancelled arrangements for Cornwall, hoping that the next fortnight would at least compensate us for a lost siesta. We dared not hope for too much. On the trail of an unknown, dead photographer and his family we might not find anything at all. The boxes of negatives might, in the end, provide only a few handfuls of pictures.

Our new plans for what was left of the summer holiday were twofold. I had already made contact prints[2] from some of the negatives, pictures of the house and of local places that I knew. Armed with the contact prints, we would trace the sites of identifiably Yorkshire pictures and explore the possibilities of the phrase, 'Atkinson, Huby'.

This phrase, for all its brevity, was not a complete enigma to us. Huby, a substantial dormitory 'village' for the well-to-do, lies beneath Armscliffe Crag, nine miles north of Leeds, between Harrogate and Otley. Getting there was, then, no problem for us and we made first for the graveyard. Huby's church, a

Methodist chapel it turned out to be, stood out at the top of the village; but there were no graves in the long grass of the churchyard. Huby despatched its dead elsewhere.

Two neighbouring villages, Rigton to the north-east and Weeton to the south, seemed likely recipients. Rigton church certainly had tombs, rows and rows of them, but, in a long and vain search through the ranks of the Victorian 'departed', the 'deceased', 'laid to rest' and the merely 'fallen asleep', we first realised what patience we would need.

At Weeton church, however, we were luckier. This substantial piece of Victorian Gothic, built on the whim of Lord Harewood, stands beautifully secluded but is clearly the servant of a prosperous community. In the corner of the churchyard, distinctively white and picked out in the sun, was a sundial inscribed to the memory of one Alfred William Atkinson (Plate 16) and his wife, Polly. Was this our man? At this point the story would begin to turn full circle.

The date of Atkinson's death, as late as 1945, was a surprise. We had assumed he had died long before, at the time the photographs were taken. As it was, he did not live to a very great age but his life stretched from the assassination of Abraham Lincoln to the destruction of Hiroshima. And he took his first photograph in the decade of which Soames Forsyte said, 'In my belief the world reached the highest point in the 1880s and will never reach it again'.

We stood at the graveside for a few minutes, since, in a superficially poignant way, it meant something to us now, having seen the family alive in the photographs. However, there was no sign that anyone still commemorated the Atkinsons' deaths with propitiatory flowers and we wondered where to go next. Who else could put flesh on the bones?

We looked for the name of the churchwarden and found he lived close by. If he were an old man, he might even have known the Atkinsons himself. He came to the door in response to our knock wearing baggy khaki shorts and sandals without socks. He was old enough to have been himself middle-aged when Alfred Atkinson died. His manner towards us was strangely reluctant; I thought at first it might be because those who come asking questions often have ulterior motives. But the real reason soon became obvious: the Atkinsons, he said with regret, were 'chapel folk'. They only trespassed on the hospitality of the established church by taking up space in the graveyard. They had devoted their lives—and, we suspected, their money—to Huby's Methodist chapel. To Weeton they bequeathed only their dust. Nevertheless, the churchwarden did give us a 'lead': Mr Atkinson had lived at Fir Tree House, Huby, but the house was, he said, empty and soon to be auctioned.

Back in Huby village Messrs Adair, Davy and Mosley, chartered surveyors of Leeds, had ensured that we would find the house. Their strident hoarding advertised the sale of the house by auction two weeks later. The house faced the village post-office-cum-general-store, its frontage surprisingly modest in view of what the photographs had shown us of the life which once surrounded it. From the road we could see a stone-built cottage badly masked by an ugly coach-house and the overgrown hedges that cluttered the narrow strip of front garden. This public façade, however, was deceptively plain.

We walked through the lower gate and swung round the semi-circular drive. The garden and house were decayed but the photographs we had with us helped to people the scene as it once was. The house itself had clearly grown back from the road in stages, keeping abreast of the family fortunes. The later additions were more aspiring in style than the original cottage and the result was a curious mixture of village bluntness overlaid with suburban pomp, like a ploughman in morning dress. Some windows were plain; others tricked out with leaded Art Nouveau panes. Soiled net curtains hung in the main bay. In a very physical way the building no longer knew which way to look: the original front door had opened on to the village street but a new, more imposing stone vestibule had been added on another side where the family could view its own private splendour. This grander façade had been solid backcloth in the more formal family photographs.

Inside, the house had been stripped and much of what remained was peeling. There were acres of mahogany and dark-varnished woodwork, and ornate plaster mouldings cracked and stained by the damp. A few small piles of dust and junk had been cursorily swept into corners; among them we found a small piece of ruby-coloured glass that would have

been used in a photographic darkroom. There was, however, only one really human reminder: a tiny pair of old lady's patent leather shoes, toes and heels together, punctiliously well-mannered on the bare boards of a huge empty bedroom.

The room itself looked out on an acre of garden whose wild profusion now mocked the polite and ordered world it once served. Neat shrubs had grown into grotesque giants, swamping the borders and sprawling over terraces. Rhododendrons had twisted their way across the lawn and now threatened the sundial where, in the photographs, a mother and her children had paraded in their party clothes (Plate 17). Nearby, weeds and shoulder-high grass competed in a game of no rules where once shuttlecocks flew (Plate 18). In the far corner of the garden, behind hydrangeas and the broken skeleton of a pergola, gleamed white timbers; we picked our way through spikes of foxgloves and rosebay willowherb for a closer look. There were two structures: one a summerhouse which surveyed the croquet lawn and where the less active had retired to take tea (Plate 19). Now the timbers were rotted, a drift of dead leaves hid the floor and brambles strayed through the broken leaded lights. Next to the summerhouse was the shadowy hut with vaguely oriental lattice-work; here the children had played out their mock-Japanese tea parties (Plate 20). It was not difficult to imagine squeals of girlish delight.

Someone from the village had been watching our prowl round the grounds and now she called to us from the other side of the garden. It was an understandable request for us to explain ourselves. We did so and reassured the lady that we were not vandals, nor, sadly, prospective purchasers. In return she told us what she knew of the recent history of the house and the owner of those patent leather shoes. We learned of the death of a 'Miss Kathleen', aged seventy-five in the January of that year. She had survived alone in Fir Tree House where she had lived since she was a girl. During her last few years the people of the village had taken care of her; they cooked and cleaned and helped sort out her confusion when the past was more real to her than the present. Miss Kathleen was apparently, however, no recluse: she roamed the village for a chat or something interesting to watch. Her appearance was sometimes untimely or odd. One might have to ignore the ill-matched bedroom slipper on one foot and the laced shoe on the other or the *crêpe de Chine* blouse over striped pyjama bottoms. If she called on a villager, it might be in the small hours with a piece of cake or someone else's dog.

There was in this picture a suspicion of sentimentality. Perhaps the village had created for this solitary maid the role they wanted her to play and an image they could remember with affection. When she died, the contents of her house fell under the hammer. They realised £15,000.

The second part of our summer search took us away from Huby to follow the Atkinsons' Yorkshire travels. This was more a series of separate skirmishes than a single campaign but some general impressions remain. There was usually reason for regret—not simply that things had gone but that the changes since the time of the photographs were invariably for the worse.

The route took us first into the greener parts of Leeds where Victorians took their week-end walks. The country quiet survives but only just and hardly at Roundhay Park Waterfall (Plate 21). In 1808, Thomas Nicholson at Roundhay had a house built by Clark of York and a quarry on his land transformed into a lake—Waterloo Lake. When Alfred Atkinson photographed the artificially-constructed outfall in about 1890, the Nicholson estate had been bought by Leeds Corporation for its citizens for £139,000. We naturally assumed that such a picturesque fall would be well known or, at least, easy to find. However, in a complete circuit of the lake, we walked right past it; our attention was drawn to the garish public swimming-pool immediately below. New railings at the top of the waterfall also deprived us of the precarious adventure shared by the schoolboys in Alfred Atkinson's picture. And to take a modern picture from the same viewpoint as his, we had to clamber over wire and push through undergrowth and bushes. Over the years the waterfall had become a predictable depository for litter, old timber, rusted wheels and even a galvanised milk crate. There was a stench and too many flies. And when we saw the place in the middle of a dry summer the water, which in Atkinson's picture drifts milkily downwards, only dribbled through the moss.

A second Leeds photograph took us a few miles north to Meanwood. In the spring of 1887 Alfred Atkinson caught a selfconscious group of friends perched on a rustic bridge over Meanwood Beck (Plate 22). The men contrive to be casual while the youngsters are overawed by the occasion. One, especially, stands rigidly to attention and is betrayed by his clothes—round-bellied, knock-kneed and pigeon-toed. Together the four have brought their good manners and their smart clothes from suburban Leeds to impose on the countryside; they dare the mud to dull the impeccable shine on their shoes. If they stood there now, they would be disturbed by the traffic on the Leeds ring-road a hundred yards away, close enough to leave its mark. When we found the place, there was an old tyre half-submerged in the middle of the stream. Finding the site was not easy: it had changed almost beyond recognition. The bridge had gone, the gate, the steps and also the ford. Several trees had fallen and the stream ran a different course. Parts of the old bridge supports we found collapsed in the weeds on the bank. And under inches of silt were the cobbles on which the carts used to cross the stream.

From Leeds to York. Here we expected an easier search and a story with a happier end. More than any other city in the north, York preserves its past in buildings and streets. Petergate (Plate 23) and Shambles (Plate 24) have changed their dress since Alfred Atkinson's time but their characters lie deeper than that and still survive. One of the pictures, however, proved elusive (Plate 25)—a typical street of cobbles overhung by half-timbered gables, a street which everyone we asked, of course, knew well. But no one was right. We felt the local library archives were the place to look and, sure enough, in a faded sepia print there was the street, pictured from the other end but undeniably the same. Its name baffled us—Little Shambles—until a city plan showed that it had been demolished to make way for the open market place.

This research left us with mixed feelings about Alfred Atkinson's picture of Little Shambles. Certainly it had aesthetic charm; narrow streets frame themselves in pictures and create their own highlights and shadows; and we all see quaintness in ancient and dilapidated buildings. However, in the library at York we also learned a sadder, human side to the history of Little Shambles. It was in such streets that Seebohm Rowntree, in his seminal study of York in 1901, found one third of the city's people in a state of 'primary poverty'—that is, underfed. Library records showed us that some of the slums in Little Shambles, condemned under the Clearance Order of 1937, were not demolished until 1951.

Before leaving York, we wanted to date the photograph of Little Shambles. Our clue was a detail in the picture: on a hoarding behind the women whose gossip the picture has prolonged, the North Eastern Railway proudly claims to be going places: 'York to Bridlington in sixty minutes' (Plate 25a). That was a fact new enough at the time to be boasted on advertisements. We decided to consult the timetables at the National Railway Museum, which is, conveniently, in York. Unfortunately, the Technical Information Officer had not a complete collection but, by extrapolation, he guessed 1908 as the likely year for the introduction of fast trains on the new direct line through Market Weighton and Driffield. Later research also put Alfred Atkinson in York in 1908 on an official photographic excursion.

For Edwardians in York, then, the sea at Bridlington was only an hour away. We travelled by car in 1975 and it took more than an hour on the busy summer roads. For the city people of Alfred Atkinson's time the railway offered a means of escape and they flocked on excursions to the coast. For many Bridlington (Plate 26) offered a rare or perhaps first sight of the sea, although even the most sentimental can hardly have matched Charlotte Brontë's response when she gazed from the promenade half a century earlier, in 1839:

> She was overpowered; she could not speak till she had shed some tears; she signed for her friend to leave her and walk on; this she did for a few steps ... and joined her as soon as she thought she might without inflicting pain; her eyes were red and swollen, she was still trembling, but she submitted to be led to where the view was less impressive ...

There is still cause to weep at Bridlington today as, while the south beach is still unspoiled, there are acres of plastic and neon fun around the harbour. So we were more anxious than Charlotte Brontë to move on. We already knew that the Atkinsons were no strangers to the bays and harbours on the Yorkshire coast, from Bridlington itself to as far north as Runswick (Plate 27). Some of them, like Scarborough, were originally fashionable spas and resorts which, until the coming of the railway, attracted mainly the well-to-do; others, like Runswick Bay, were less showy, and the inhabitants found their quiet lives disturbed by city people in search of romantic reminders of the pre-industrialised north. Alfred Atkinson took pictures of them all, large or small, flamboyant or coy. Sometimes he recorded truly indigenous life before its obliteration by the tourist trade. Scarborough had been taken over long before. We drove there next for an audience with this 'Queen of English Watering Places', as it is called in Black's *Picturesque Guide to Yorkshire* of 1864.

How the Atkinsons spent their holiday time at Scarborough one can only guess; the pictures are mere glimpses. One, taken about 1890, (Plates 28 and 28a) shows Alfred Atkinson's parents, dressed to the nines, taking the air on one of the paths to the south beach. They clearly appreciated the resorts alfresco attractions. If the Atkinsons stayed at an expensive hotel, such as The Crown, full board would have cost 8*s*. 6*d*. per day (plus 1*s*. 6*d*. for 'attendance'; full board for servants 4*s*. 6*d*.). Elsewhere, more modestly, 5*s*. was the going rate. Perhaps the Atkinsons took the waters; if so, they were advised to rise early: 'The best time for taking the waters is before breakfast'. Admission to the spa cost 6*d*. per day—with extras: 'A good band of music is engaged during the season'. Nowadays Scarborough sells herself more cheaply. Even The Crown will do you mushrooms on toast. Like most who come down in the world, Scarborough cannot afford to be proud but there are reminders of a more splendid past in the cliff-top façades and the gardens above the South Bay (Plate 29).

The road from Scarborough to Whitby was for us a devious one. *En route* we hoped to find what was left of Rigg Mill. In Alfred Atkinson's photograph of it (Plate 30) the waterwheel had already, in 1893, settled into picturesque decay. Its paddles could hardly have withstood the force of the mill stream even a century ago. Unfortunately, the mill was well enough known in Alfred Atkinson's time for him not to locate it for us. Our square-by-square scrutiny of maps of Yorkshire had thrown up two Rigg Mills, one within six miles of Whitby. We did not know in advance exactly where to find the mill since its name covered half a mile of map space. However, we already knew that Atkinson did not stray far from roads. He preferred beaten tracks to forging them himself. And the elegant ladies in Atkinson's picture of Rigg Mill had surely not trailed through the mud.

We were, then, surprised to find that directions to Rigg Mill led us into the middle of fields (Plate 31) and we might have despaired but for the arrival of a landrover with the mill's new occupants. Mr and Mrs Poskitt have retired into Eden and are rightly keen to keep Paradise their own. They said that in earlier times Rigg Mill had been a fashionable tea-garden; we found the tea and the welcome less public but still very warm. We were right in supposing that the wheel had gone. And we learned that the great Victorian photographer, Frank Sutcliffe, had thought the place worth more than one visit.

Frank Sutcliffe's is the name most Yorkshire people associate first with Victorian photography. His international fame at the end of last century made Whitby the 'Photographer's Mecca' and with some sense of awe we turned to what used to be the fifth port in the land. Even in 1896, however, Sutcliffe complained that a ship was a 'curiosity' in Whitby; in his time ships were certainly outnumbered by photographers whose cameras were 'exceeded only by the numbers of sand on the shore.'

Sutcliffe's pictures document Whitby's sad, sea change. Fifty years before almost every village down the Yorkshire coast had its fleet of cobles, the smallest and most beautiful of British inshore boats. The shape pre-dates the design of modern power boats by decades. Clinker-built and carrying a narrow lug sail, cobles can be rowed with oars on a single thole pin. A few cobles still work today but their nets are threatened by bigger trawlers sailing too close to the shore. Fleets of family boats appeal to us now as reminders of a time when the little man could be big in being complete in himself. But Sutcliffe's pictures were tinged with regret even in his own time.

Alfred Atkinson, less professional in his way and flattering Sutcliffe by imitation, was more detached. He took what was there (Plates 32–5) and recorded it without any self-consciously romantic poses. Atkinson's tracks at Whitby were easy for us to follow although new warehouses and crowds often obscured his views from us. Both obstacles were reminders that Whitby had lost its seclusion and much of its charm.

One of Alfred Atkinson's pictures we knew would involve a quieter search. North of Whitby, in the woods above Sandsend Bay, stands Mulgrave Castle, mock castle rather, since the 'castle' is only an embellishment on an eighteenth-century house. The real castle (Plate 36), or its twelfth-century remains, are now only overgrown heaps in the grounds. A charming old lady, sitting outside her cottage in a garden of impossible colour, told us the grounds were shut; so we had to leave the ruins to decay undisturbed.

The last stop before we turned south and left the coast was at Runswick (Plates 37–9), which clings precariously in a cleft of the cliffs above its bay, in defiance, one might think, of the law of gravity. Nature prevailed, in fact, in the seventeenth century when the entire village slid into the sea. The new owners of holiday homes, however, seem confident enough: they pay upwards of £20,000 for a foothold among the rocks and spend fortunes transforming it into Ingleneuk, Sea Cliffe or Binnacle Cottage. Despite the cliff falls, the villagers enjoy the steep disarray in which seaward neighbours can't block the light, but offer instead a view down their chimneys. There is much work going on, transforming old world into olde worlde, with Dickensian pane and Georgian bow. Part-time sailors and fishermen abound. They remember the true natives with affection and cherish old pictures of Runswick but the spirit, like the pictures, has faded.

The journey home to Wakefield we punctuated with two stops after crossing the North Yorkshire Moors. Rievaulx (Plate 40), Helmsley (Plate 41) and Duncombe (Plate 42) are sufficiently close to count as one stop and offer a range of abbey, castle and hall. Rievaulx Abbey and Helmsley Castle taught us the same thing: the serious science of modern archaeology may have preserved the sites from further decay but has destroyed the Gothic atmosphere they once had. Modern experts may dismiss that as irrelevant but the Victorians found it invigorating and heady. They revered the awesome

Spirit of the Past, who lived in ivy on mouldering piles. Strangely, they were also happy to picnic or play tennis on the turf with no sense of being out of place.

No one serves tea or aces at Helmsley now and children and dogs are kept off the grass. We heard an earnest schoolteacher parent rehearsing his four-year-old son in a catechism of the parts of medieval forts. In the middle of a month-long heat-wave the poor infant had no taste for subjects as dry as this. An ice-cream would have been far more alluring.

In the adjoining Duncombe Park we were prepared not to find much at all. In Alfred Atkinson's photograph (Plate 42) the hall had clearly suffered a singular catastrophe. Only the shored-up façades remained. In fact, what we found was a building completely restored—a magnificent example of Neo-Classical architecture less than a hundred years old and put to new use as an exclusive girls' school. Much of the original structure, built in 1713 by William Wakefield to a design by Vanbrugh, was assimilated into the new structure whose straight face hides the human story that must lie behind the fire of 1879.

From Duncombe to Nidderdale Head is only forty miles but the developers of Howstean Beck, our last halt, would have us believe we had been transported much further. They call the place, 'Little Switzerland'. Blasé modern tourists, who know the real thing, may be unimpressed by the claim. For Victorian travellers, however, Howstean Gorge, with its spectacular erosion and precarious overhang, boasted a taste of Alpine adventure. There still stands at the entrance, in the most rural of settings, an ornate but rusting turnstile, forged by Bailey's of Salford and lugged over the Pennines in the days when even the most functional things were made decorative. The turnstile testifies to how many Victorians made the long journey up the dale to prove for themselves the claim for Howstean's continental splendour.

Alfred Atkinson and his party, visiting Howstean before 1890, supplemented the thrills of slippery rocks and dizzy bridges with cumbersome long dresses (Plate 43) and unwieldy plate camera and tripod. Even modern equipment with fast lens and fast film finds the gloom difficult to pierce except on the brightest of days. Atkinson's subjects would have had to freeze for a minute or more, which explains why they stare from the picture like men carved out of stone (Plate 44). Isaac Atkinson, Alfred's brother, props himself nonchalantly against a tree; he seems to have no fears for the thirty-foot drop below.

We arrived back in Wakefield feeling that the holiday had been successful both in itself and in promising more to come. We knew at least that the photographs were only illustrations in a longer story. The first chapters closed at the end of the summer holidays, when I set up a private exhibition of Alfred Atkinson's Yorkshire pictures and my own modern equivalents for comparison. That caused some excitement among my friends and they prompted me to find out more.

---

[1] Isaac Rosenberg, 'August, 1914'.

[2] Contact printing is straightforward; it simply involves putting the negative directly onto printing paper and exposing to light before developing and fixing.

1

POLLY ATKINSON, ABOUT 1890

2

3

'*Miscellaneous Boats*'

ILFRACOMBE, ABOUT 1890

4

5 to 7

'Mixed Groups' 1887–1900

(POLLY ATKINSON, NÉE HEBDEN APPEARS IN
THEM ALL)

5

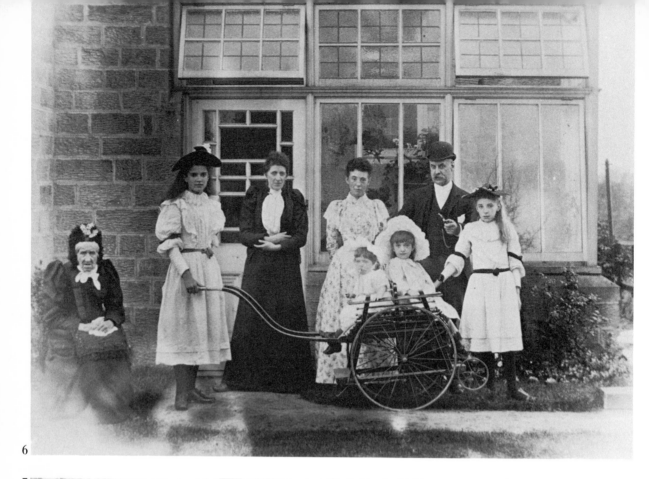

6

7

8

'*Accidental pleasures of holidays and outings*' 1890–1920

9

'Figures posed in landscapes or caught in lanes'

HENRY ATKINSON ON THE RIVER WHARFE AT BOLTON, 1890

12

GLEN ESK, NEAR WHITBY, 1895

'Recognisable beauty spots in Yorkshire'

13

KILNSEY CRAG, ABOUT 1890

OVERLEAF: 14 and 15
ROBIN HOOD'S BAY, ABOUT 1890

15

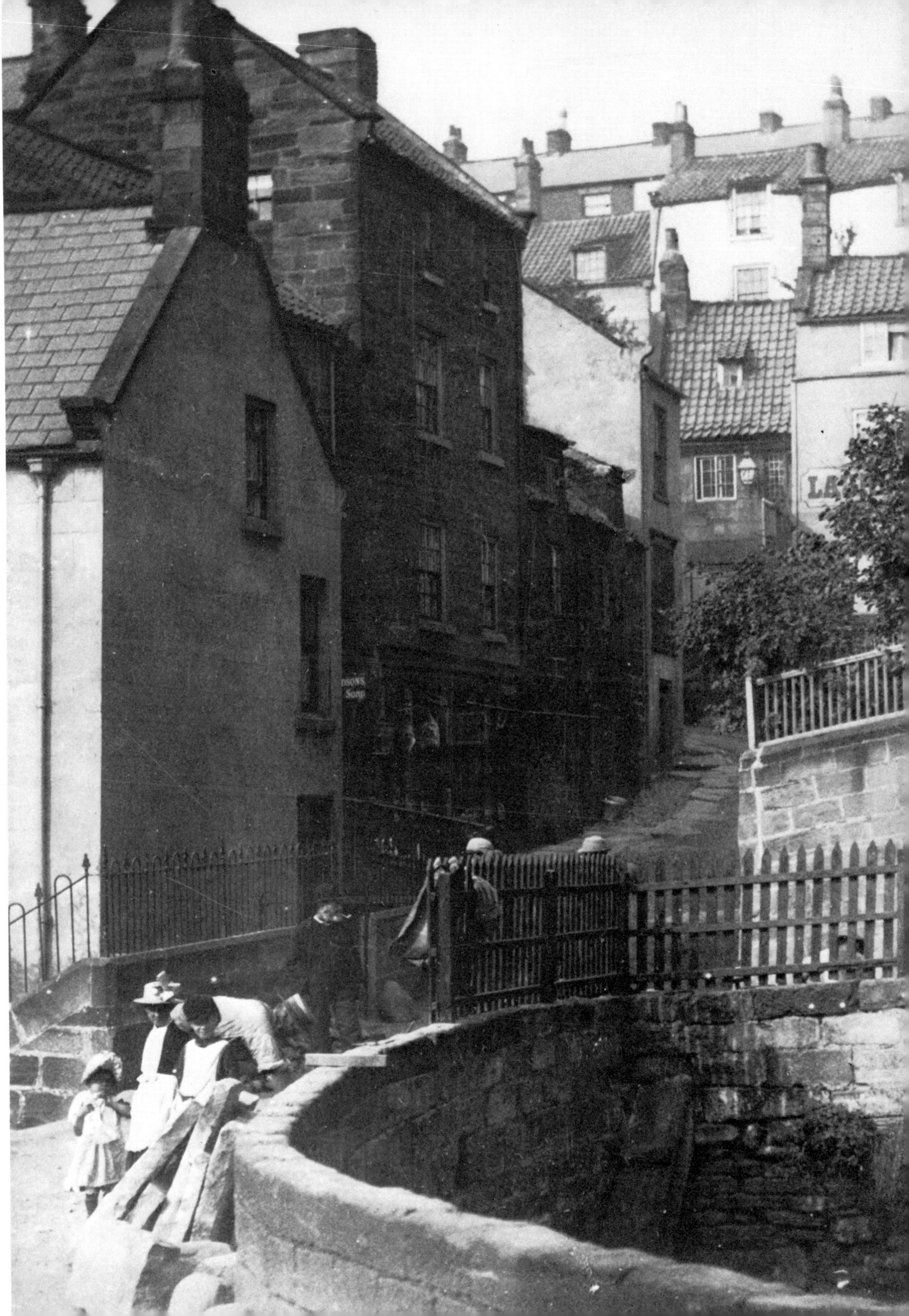

ALFRED WILLIAM ATKINSON, 1864–1945   POLLY ATKINSON, ABOUT 1910

'Where shuttlecocks flew'

HUBY, 1905

'Tea in the arbour'

THE ATKINSON FAMILY WITH
MRS TAIT OF BRADFORD,
AT HUBY, 1906

'Children had played out mock-Japanese tea parties'

ROUNDHAY PARK WATERFALL, LEEDS, 1893

MEANWOOD BECK, LEEDS, 1887
(WILLIAM THOMAS HEBDEN ON THE LEFT)

23

24

25

YORK, 1908:

23 LOWER PETERGATE
24 THE SHAMBLES
25 LITTLE SHAMBLES
25a DETAIL

OVERLEAF:
26 BRIDLINGTON HARBOUR, ABOUT 1890

HENRY AND ELLEN ATKINSON AT SCARBOROUGH,
1889

28a DETAIL

29

THE GARDENS ABOVE THE SOUTH BAY, SCARBOROUGH, 1889
RIGG MILL, NEAR WHITBY, 1893

30

31

32

32 to 35   WHITBY, ABOUT 1895

31   THE MILL STREAM, 1893

34

35

37

38

37 to 39   RUNSWICK BAY, ABOUT 1890

40

RIEVAULX ABBEY, ABOUT 1890

41

HELMSLEY CASTLE, ABOUT 1890

42

DUNCOMBE HALL, ABOUT 1890

'*Little Switzerland*' HOWSTEAN BECK, 1889 (AND 44 OVERLEAF)

3

2

IN THE DARK AND THE SOUTH

IN THE EVENINGS of autumn 1975, I directed my attention to Alfred Atkinson's negatives themselves. I had turned only a few into prints; many of them I had as yet merely glanced at and most I still could not identify. The first, inglorious task was to contact print all 650. I had the rudimentary technique to cope with the job even in amateur surroundings where the darkroom doubles as a bedroom. Such a large number of negatives, however, was a test of patience and I cut corners to save time, grouping two or four negatives of the same contrast and density and exposing them simultaneously on a large sheet of paper. Even so, a batch of thirty or forty was enough for a full evening, including the washing and drying of them. At least the work threw up a few surprises: some apparently modest negatives only showed their character in the positive print. Little Shambles (Plate 25) is a good example; the negative is very dense and lacking in contrast—it looks simply misty and grey.

Seeing the quality of the contact prints, I naturally wanted to enlarge them. Examining details with a glass was rewarding but frustrating. Without an enlarger to handle negatives of that size, I could only enlarge small sections of negatives to explore details—distant figures, especially. It was exciting to see mere specks on the negative grow into people or legible writing. It was, however, a tantalising time, having to imagine the overall effect from one piece of the jigsaw. Fortunately, a professional photographer in Leeds, with an eye for the history of his business, offered me the use of a veteran enlarger which could handle negatives the size of window panes and which itself belonged to the world of Atkinson's photographs.

Made—perhaps 'built' would be more appropriate—in about 1920, this Kodak 'Autofocus' is a solid job. It has a huge hemispherical lamphouse and needs a bulb that would heat up a room; so there is a primitive chimney to disperse the heat and the smoke. The lens is magnificently set in brass, although its outer glass surfaces have suffered the odd scratch. Focusing is a problem: it takes two hands and considerable strength to shift the mechanism and that makes it hard to look at the projected picture. Unused for many years, the electrical parts were dangerous but, rewired, the enlarger now performs well and, partly through old age, imbues prints with a diffused 'period' look (Plate 81).

Alfred Atkinson's pictures had probably never before been seen any larger than album size and, since the negatives themselves were the size of modern enprints, they would enlarge to a size that would fill the wall of a room without hopeless loss of definition. These were pictures one could step into. Plates I had ignored after a first cursory glance now gave up secrets even the photographer possibly never knew.

One picture, for example, Atkinson took in the Yorkshire Dales village of Malham in about 1890 (Plate 45). When I first saw the negative, I thought it unexceptional and empty, except that the carriages outside the inn suggested how inaccessible were most parts of the countryside except to an affluent few. However, when Atkinson set up his tripod on the bank of the river which runs through the village, he unwittingly caught a much more significant piece of social history which is easily overlooked without an enlargement. Tucked away in the distance, below where the Youth Hostel now stands, a grimly-dressed group take their sober enjoyment in the forecourt of Clark's Temperance Hotel (Plate 45a). An audience of two young locals looks on, perhaps in awe of the severity.

That sent me off to read about drink and the Victorians. Such temperance excursions were organised by reformers as a rival attraction to those more notorious leisure activities which seemed to offer the chance of drinking, gambling and fighting. From their inception temperance societies backed temperance hotels, though some proprietors used the name to cloak dark practices. Even some brothels became nominal 'temperance' hotels to allay public suspicion. Commercially, of course, temperance hotels could not really compete. In that characteristically Victorian struggle between moderation and excess, soul and body, mortal appetites won; temperance hotels offered their limited refreshment to a more and more limited few. Mercy W. Clark, however, of Malham, squarely faced her disreputable competitors in the Lister's Arms across the road; Beauty defied the Beast. She was, fortunately, twice blest: her real living must have been made in her adjoining grocery shop. It is most unlikely that she ran a bordello for dalesmen.

In another of Alfred Atkinson's excursions, through Kilburn in north Yorkshire, in about 1910, he stopped to photograph the prettiest cottage in the village (Plate 46). It would mean nothing more to him then, since its occupant was at the time and until 1915 an obscure jobbing carpenter making wagons for local farmers. Nor did the photograph mean any more to us when we drove to Kilburn to confront the present owner with a picture of his house as it had been. The cottage was easy to find: it had become since 1915 the focus of the village. In that year its occupant was commissioned by the Abbot of Ampleforth to make a graveyard cross. Thereafter he furnished the library at Ampleforth College; this and other commissions, including work at York Minster, spread the reputation of this remarkable craftsman in oak. His carving was famous for its quality and identified by a mouse motif on every piece. Robert 'Mouse' Thompson founded a business which is still run by his grandsons. They have inevitably transferred to a modern, brick-built factory which stands incongruously and noisily behind the village houses but the original cottage is still used as a showroom. The furniture sells all over the world.

Discoveries like these brightened the tedium of long and repetitive hours in the darkroom. When the contact prints were done, I began to feel that there was sufficient in the photographs to interest others who hadn't the excitement of discovery to keep them

involved. I knew there was a danger of overvaluing the photographs for the pleasure they had given me. I still did not know whether such collections were unusual.

With these mixed feelings I wrote to the local Arts Association for a more objective view. The Visual Arts Officer actually shared my enthusiasm, despite the amateurish prints I then had to show, and suggested an exhibition. So I returned with a sense of urgency to the question of the photographer and his family, about whom I knew very little, except through the pictures.

What other routes would lead inside the Atkinsons' life and home? One was through books of social history and anthologies of contemporary documents. I ransacked colleagues' bookshelves and read history with a rare sense of purpose. The books built a framework around the family, a context to place them in. But concepts such as 'the rise of the self-made middle-class family' made the story typical not unique. The Atkinsons were more than historical examples. I needed a closer look.

In the meantime, there were more of the Atkinsons' holidays to follow, this time to the south-west. The Atkinsons loved Devon and travelled there at the big moments of their lives. Mr and Mrs Atkinson spent their honeymoon at Clovelly; in Lynmouth they recovered from the shock of the death of their first daughter. Later the whole family spent summers in Torquay.

Alfred Atkinson made albums of prints to preserve memories of these visits and that gave Christine and me a reason for taking our postponed holiday to the south-west. Over Christmas 1975, we scoured Devon as we had done Yorkshire a few months before.

The long journey south is now deceptively easy and the monotonous motorway miles gave time to reflect on the quality of expedition that must have attended such long journeys in Victorian times, despite the growth of the railways. Once off the train, the Atkinsons took to sedate horse and carriage (Plate 47). At least they were less prone to mechanical faults as we had reason to rue when the car boiled on Porlock Hill and later broke down. We came to rest, fortunately, at Lynmouth.

Although I had never been there before, Lynmouth was a landmark in my childhood. The floods that tore through the town in August 1952, were one of those events outside the immediate world which caught my imagination before I was of an age to be reading newspapers. Such events—and they were usually disasters—seemed on a scale above the mundane, more suited to the epic than the novel. Alfred Atkinson's pictures (Plates 48 and 49), therefore, have a special nostalgia. Their idyllic atmosphere is touched with irony.

Before the flood, Lynmouth had a continental flavour. Many of the literary figures of the Romantic movement saw in it a reminder of their Grand Tours. Hazlitt and Coleridge were there; Southey even bought a cottage. Almost a century later the prospect of the village and the wooded coombe of Glen Lyn (Plate 50) were photographed unchanged. Since then the peace has been shattered and, like a patient after an operation, the village now all too eagerly displays its scars. As you enter Glen Lyn to inspect the flood damage, a notice points to the lack of commercialisation and demands your forty pence.

Clovelly, along the coast, (Plate 51) took nothing from us and gave a great deal more. This 'mighty sing'lar and pretty place' is best seen through the eyes of Captain Jorgan (a joint creation of Wilkie Collins and Charles Dickens in 'A Message from the Sea' in Dickens's *Christmas Stories*):

> There was no road in it, there was no wheeled vehicle in it. There was not a level yard in it. From the sea beach to the cliff top two irregular rows of white houses . . . twisting here and there and there and here rose and you climbed . . . by the staves between, some six feet wide or so, and made of sharp, irregular stones . . . the pier was musical with the wash of the sea, the creaking of capstans and windlasses, and the airy fluttering of little vanes and sails. The rough, sun-bleached boulders of the shore were brown with the drying of nets . . .

In the days when the Atkinsons knew Clovelly, boats brought coal and limestone across from South Wales. The lime kiln is still there but not many traces of the isolated community life that first attracted the Victorian tourists. Similar villages in Cornwall, notably Newlyn and St Ives, as reminders of pre-industrialised England, became artists' colonies in the 1890s. In the *Art Journal* (1889)

Alice Meynell felt inspired to write of Newlyn:

> A fisherman in a jersey is one of the few modern Englishmen not burlesqued by his garments. And the man who wears a blue jersey generally holds his head in the manner of one familiar with the sky and with horizons.

Alfred Atkinson did not patronise the fishermen but took what was offered. When he pointed his camera at a string of sailors resting outside the coal bunkers on the harbour-side (Plate 52), they showed most shades of response, from the indifferent, through the reluctant, to the proud. Atkinson also took his camera into the labyrinth of cobbled passageways that border the main ramp from the harbour (Plate 53). There he photographed a cottage which, eighty years later when we were there, was owned by a man who had served forty years on the Clovelly lifeboat, the 'William Cantrell Ashley', which first slipped into the sea in 1925. As a boy he used to admire the strength of the youngest men in Atkinson's picture, by then in their middle age. He was, when we met him, still wearing sea boots and guernsey, because the sea had been his life.

At Clovelly the rain also came and drove us to Torquay. There the winter wet gave the place some of the dull sadness it owned as a refuge for consumptives over a century ago. It emerged as a watering place from a tiny fishing village during the Napoleonic Wars when the English fleet anchored in Torbay, awaiting its orders. For a time, at least, it attracted people of fashion when in 1815 HMS *Bellerophon* anchored there with Napoleon captive on board. Thereafter the town settled back into a home for weak lungs. In its sheltered warmth, 'Palm Courts' were more than false claims.

By the turn of the century, however, spitting pots were less common in hotels. The healthy and gay now far outnumbered those who came to die of a decline. During the Edwardian years Torquay really prospered from the enterprise of Sir Lawrence Palk, an earlier Lord of the Manor with ideas for the place. Of the Great War's tidal wave not so much as a ripple splashed on the beach. The hotels, Grand and Imperial, basked in apparently unclouded sun (Plate 54).

During these twenty years, as their children grew up, the Atkinsons were often beside the south Devon sea. As the photographs show (Plates 54–8), the English had not yet reverted to worshipping the sun. Most clothes for the beach, in fact, armed the wearer against the smallest shaft of sun. Bathing, however, was 'in' and had been for two hundred years. Fortunately for the Atkinsons, the practice of drinking sea water (the usual dose was half a pint) had died out and people took their dips for pleasure more than for cure.

It even seems that by Edwardian times bathing suits were actually designed for the job. Earlier Victorian designers did not consider that their elaborate frills were to be immersed in water. There is a story of a stir when, in the 1890s, a girl of sixteen swam over four hundred yards wearing 'not only all the ordinary undergarments of a lady, including corsets, but also a heavy, fishwife's, serge dress, boots, hat and gloves, carrying in one hand a huge scarlet twill umbrella opened and in the other a large bouquet of somewhat gaudy flowers.'[1]

Equally bizarre to modern eyes are the clothes which Victorian parents (the Atkinsons, too) asked their children to wear, even at play. They smothered and encumbered, displaying an image of children that parents wanted to believe in—their offspring as adults in miniature. At least at the seaside Victorian parents pandered to their children's tastes: donkey rides and sandcastles had been common a century or more. Cute as she is with bucket and spade in her father's photograph (Plate 58), Kathleen Atkinson is not now likely to prompt speculation as serious as William Hutton's (of Scarborough, 1803): 'To observe the little animals, in the greatest degree of health and spirits, fabricating their pies in the sand, is a treat for the philosopher.'

In this way Alfred Atkinson's pictures helped recall the spirit of holidays past. But holidays are extrovert times: we measure them out in things done. We wanted a more intimate view of the Atkinsons 'at home'.

[1] Quoted in Ruth Manning Sanders, *Seaside England*, 1951.

45

45a

MALHAM, ABOUT 1890; 45A DETAIL

46

ROBERT THOMPSON'S COTTAGE AT KILBURN,
ABOUT 1900

'The Atkinsons took to sedate horse and carriage'

POLLY ATKINSON HEAVILY CHAPERONED
(LEFT) IN DEVON, ABOUT 1890

47

48

LYNMOUTH TOWER AND HARBOUR, 1897

49

50

GLEN LYN, 1897

51 and 52 (overleaf)
CLOVELLY HARBOUR, ABOUT 1890

57 COCKINGTON FORGE, ABOUT 1914

58 KATHLEEN ATKINSON AT THE SEASIDE,
    ABOUT 1901

3

CRESCENDO...GRANDIOSO

ON MY FIRST visit to Huby I learned that Alfred Atkinson's grandson, Godfrey Linfoot, had acted as executor on the death of his aunt, Miss Kathleen. I thought that interesting things might have passed through his hands and shown him something of the leisurely times in the house. I wrote to Mr Linfoot and he invited me to Faceby in Cleveland, where he now lives. One icy weekend, in February 1976, I drove to the village, amost cut off in the lee of the Cleveland hills. In fact, my hopes had been too modest: when Godfrey Linfoot walked into his aunt's house, he found it crammed full with parcels. In her eccentric declining years, Miss Kathleen had obsessively hoarded whatever in passing whim had caught her eye. As if for an eternal game of pass the parcel, she meticulously wrapped each bundle in several layers and secreted it away. All the packages had to be opened after her death in the search for her will. They contained trinkets and trivia: from small pieces of silver to shopping lists.

Most things had to be sold or thrown away but Mr Linfoot did keep documents, especially those which helped piece together the family's earlier history: certificates of marriage, birth and death; account books and invoices; letters and, finest of all, photographic albums containing his grandfather's own prints. Names, dates and places—the landmarks of lives—were just what I needed to map out the family territory. I could now locate the Atkinsons in local history library records. My Easter holiday seemed to shrink in length; most of it would be spent in Leeds City Library, fitting surroundings for the work. With its Corinthian columns, tiled mosaics and brass handrails, the library is a magnificent expression of civic pride and its fussy dignity the very stuff of the years I wanted to explore. For three weeks I lost myself in the depths of the local history section with street and trade directories and other Victorian records, some from

Mr Linfoot. In this sort of sleuthing even the simplest pieces of evidence—a name, a date or address—can be exciting. Slowly I put together those events in the Atkinsons' past before the beginning of this century which no one living can remember. The story is a classic of its time.

By the middle of the nineteenth century industry in Leeds had become a leviathan fed with huge amounts of coal and steam. In 1860 the 83 collieries in the Leeds district produced 2,459,000 tons of coal. In 1855, 102 works turned out between six and seven million pounds worth of woollen cloth. Another 12,000 employees spun and wove flax; 1,500 made worsted and silk; 8,000 were in engineering. A few were borne to shore on this tide; most struggled to stay afloat; and many went under. Drowning souls looked in vain for help in a world where the chief opponents of elementary schooling for all were the Lord Chancellor and the Archbishop of Canterbury. Where church and state failed, 'self-help' was the gospel of hope. Many had been preaching and practising the faith since the second quarter of the century.

In March 1844, for example, four young working-men in Leeds had agreed to meet weekly in each other's homes 'to improve themselves by mutual discourse'. The word had spread quickly and the four who had made shift for themselves found many more clamouring to join them. The Leeds Mutual Improvement Society, as they then called themselves, moved to a garden house in Richmond Hill; then a room in St Peter's Square. They met for two hours each evening of the week in two classes: the 'elementary' (three R's) and the 'chemical'. Each member paid a penny a week. Some were also working a ten-hour factory day. The teachers gave their services free. On Tuesday nights they talked; doubtless they set the world alight or turned it upside down. At the end of one year, at the anniversary meeting, in fact, 100 members crowded into the rented room to hear the man who had inspired them all.

Samuel Smiles had trained as a doctor in Scotland before travelling south to live in Leeds from 1838. He no longer tended the sick but turned radical journalist and encouraged the ignorant to look after themselves. This was his message to The Leeds Mutual Improvement Society:

> The education of the working classes is to be regarded in its highest aspect, not as a means of raising up a few clever and talented men into a higher rank of life, but of elevating and improving the whole class ... to make the great mass of people virtuous, well-informed, intelligent and well-conducted; and to open up to them new sources of pleasure and happiness.... What matter how much steam power we employ, if we keep man more than ever yoked to the car of toil? Man, I insist, has a right to leisure ... leisure to think, leisure to read, leisure to enjoy....

Samuel Smiles' words fell on eager ears and, as a book in 1859, *Self-Help* was one of the publishing sensations of the century. It sold 20,000 copies in its first year.

The names of that audience in Leeds are not recorded; but doubtless they converted others. Hard work and bold choices then brought fortunes to many young men. The most remarkable hero in these sagas of precocious success was Cuthbert Brodrick who, having thumbed his nose at his employers, designed Leeds Town Hall before he was thirty. Queen Victoria gave her royal assent to the new spirit abroad when she travelled north to Leeds in 1858 to open the new Town Hall. The building was clearly conceived as an inspiration to others as well as one in the eye for rival corporations; it would be 'a practical admonition to the populace of the value of beauty and art, and in the course of time men would learn to live up to it'.[1] The new edifice would also stand as a symbol of what young men of talent and initiative could achieve and many set out to follow in Brodrick's tracks to make names for themselves.

Among them was a young man from the Gascoigne estate at Aberford, outside Leeds: Henry Atkinson, Alfred Atkinson's father. In 1859, at the age of thirty-six, Henry found a partner who shared his ambition and, with David Hewson Waldby, set up as builder and joiner in the Carlton Hill district of Leeds. They also undertook to bury those whom they helped to house. Carlton Hill was a small community of terraces a few hundred yards north of the city centre, below what is now the University. There were no less than ten Carlton groves, streets, places and terraces surrounding the huge Carlton Textile Mills. By the end of the century there were also two other mills, a clothing factory and a wall-paper factory (Grove Works). To the north-east the streets looked out over the drill ground of Carlton Hill barracks. In all the intense industrial and residential acreage, there was one substantial spot of green — Queen's Square to the south, with its gardens and trees. Even that, however, was overlooked by a factory on Claypit Lane. At least Woodhouse Moor was less than a mile up the road; that was the site of most outdoor civic celebrations. On the day of the opening of Leeds Town Hall, Queen Victoria saw 32,110 schoolchildren assembled on platforms on the moor to salute her before she passed Carlton Hill on her way down to the city centre.

In a slim, black pocketbook Henry Atkinson recorded accounts in the early years of his business. In spidery hand and uncertain spelling, he inscribed the first page: 'Commensed Bussiness, April, 1859' (sic), little knowing what edifice would be built on these shaky foundations. Leeds needed houses; its population had trebled in forty years, if the official census figures show more than the corporation swallowing up other areas (1801: 15,162; 1841: 152,313). Atkinson and Waldby built substantial terraces: high-density shelter for those who serviced the industrial machine. But they also aspired to projects on a larger scale — a new co-operative store at Holbeck and extensive work on Knaresborough Town Hall, both in 1862.

In their records of 'Men's Time' sweat and endeavour are reduced to hours and cash. Six men were employed in June 1859, earning about 25s. for an average of fifty-six hours a week. In the next seven years the work force increased to twenty. Although fifty-six hours was the average working week, up to seventy hours was not unknown (for about 32s.). By the standards of the time, however,

Atkinson's men were not slaves. Only fifteen years earlier an Act had been passed forbidding employers from working children under fourteen for more than ten hours a day.

Henry Atkinson and David Waldby, of course, fared better. The business arrangement between them was a rudimentary affair. Between 1861 and 1867 Waldby received irregular payments in cash, from £1 to £40, always in round figures, in all nearly £700. This share-out of the profits has something of the schoolboy about it, like the furtive division of the fruits of an orchard raid. By 1866 Waldby had pocketed enough to leave his partner and set up independently in the trade at 3 Promenade Street, Harrogate.

On his share of the profits Henry Atkinson kept his wife, Ellen (née Backhouse) (Plate 59), and six children: Annie Backhouse, Henry George, Kate, Isaac, Alfred William and Mary Ellen. They all survived to adulthood, which in itself suggests they lived well. How well we would not know had not domestic crisis, economy drive or simple curiosity prompted Henry to keep detailed domestic accounts at the start of 1872. There is a story that he took his role as paterfamilias seriously enough not to delegate any jobs. No meal left the kitchen without his personal touch. His wife, Ellen, may have resented having the purse strings so tightly tied that no penny could be squandered on mere frippery. In April 1872, however, the accounts peter out; Henry's hold apparently slackened and there are no more glimpses into the shopping bag.

Henry Atkinson's family spent about £8 a month. They did not live extravagantly; his men took home £6 per month. The family's most frequent buys were what we would see as simple necessities: meat, bread, eggs, flour and fruit, the buying and soling of boots, and coal. No extravagance here; but they could afford brandy (4s. 3d.) and whisky (3s. 2d.) within a week, school fees (though never more than 1s. a week) and, exceptionally, the purchase of a pig for £4 from a Mr Upton.

Already, however, Henry's wealth was being stored in bricks. The houses he built were often leased and he was not afraid to exercise his landlord's rights, even issuing a notice to quit to Mr J.H. Thompson at 41 Dorrington Road. By the time of his death, in 1893, Henry had left the close community of Carlton Hill and built himself a larger house at Inglewood Terrace, Hyde Park, Leeds. For probate purposes his achievement was calculated in hard cash at £1400 11s. 7d. but the figure is misleading. Henry owned more than twenty houses in Carlton Cross Street and Inglewood Terrace which brought in an annual rent of about £450. This would have been their probate value but on the market they would have made upwards of £8,000. And this in a time when less than four per cent of the population left property worth more than £300.

With a sense of the moment, Henry Atkinson's sons gave him a funeral of befitting dignity. (In their funeral accounts the names of many who made no mark in their own lives ironically live on.) Henry's departure was much more of an occasion than his hopeful arrival in Leeds forty years before. When he came to Leeds, only Henry's family knew; when he left, the *Leeds Mercury* and *Yorkshire Post* told the world at large. He was laid to rest in Woodhouse cemetery in a 'French-polished oak coffin with flannel lining, best brass furniture, engraved plate and swansdown robe (best)'.

It was only a short journey for the cortège of four carriages and pairs across Woodhouse Moor. The family had cause to reflect on this closeness of death. Those sad acres near the city centre held over 15,000 graves. In some were families of a dozen or more people. Henry established his family's grave as he had done its fortune; friends and relatives celebrated the event with £2 10s. 5d. worth of 'provisions'. Henry himself might have begrudged his sons the expense of nearly £30 for the despatch of his dust. The next funeral in the undertaking accounts reads: 'black coffin for still-born child, attendance and cemetery fee, 9s. 6d.'.

Isaac and Alfred Atkinson, the two younger sons, took over control of the family business. Henry George, the eldest son, inherited his father's adventurous spirit and struck out on his own.[2]

Although his family had gone up in the world by moving to Inglewood Terrace, Alfred Atkinson had cause to remember some friends of his Carlton Hill days. In Dorrington Road, only a few yards from where Alfred had grown up, lived a family called Hebden. William Hebden, cabinet-maker, married Anne Goulds in 1864 (the year of Alfred Atkinson's birth). Compared to the Atkinsons', the story of the

Hebdens' children is a tragic one, though quite representative of the time. Their youngest of four lived only six months; the second lived only two years; the eldest son, William Thomas Hebden (Plate 60), having survived the uncertainties of childhood, died of diphtheria at the age of twenty; only his sister, Mary Hebden (Plate 61), lived a full life. Though she was christened Mary, she was 'Polly' to everyone. In their different ways these two eldest of the Hebden children, William Thomas and Polly, shaped Alfred Atkinson's life to a remarkable degree.

In 1884 young William Thomas Hebden set himself up in a small way as a 'Photographic Artist'. Only two of his prints survive as tangible results of his decision to stay out of the world of dirty hands and sweat. They are, appropriately, images of that genteel middle-class world that photography served: a well-dressed skating party on Roundhay Park lake, their composure now stained and faded, and a tennis tableau of his sister, Polly, and his girlfriend and cousin, Nellie Waite (Plate 62). In an artisan world William's choice of career might have seemed strange but, like the Atkinsons, the Hebdens had prospered on enterprise. Their world did not end at Carlton Hill. They owned a cottage at Huby, outside Leeds, where, at weekends and holidays, Samuel Smiles's vision of 'leisure to enjoy' became a fact. Polly played tennis and rode a bicycle, which many still saw as 'fast' pursuits in more than one sense.

The dresses with which tennis players encumbered themselves had not changed much since they had invited derision ten years before: 'A woman taking an active part in a lawn tennis competition may be compared to a swan waddling on a bowling green, for women clad in dresses of today were never intended by Providence to run.'[3] Polly Hebden also seems to have played tennis in a hat with ribbons and posies (Plate 63).

There is no surprise that the elegant misses taking up active games soon discarded the bustle and other superstructures intended to enhance or conceal. The 'new' fashion of casual blouses and long skirts, although firmly anchored at neck, wrist and ankle, was a true freedom from chains. Inevitably, this emancipation raised a few eyebrows among straighter-laced elders, who preferred to be corsetted in black (Plate 64). In fact, throughout Victorian times the black lustre dress, especially in silk, was an invaluable standby for ladies of indefinite age and shape, denoting staidness without pride. Even Mrs Manning, the murderess, kept up appearances to the last and was hanged in black satin.

In her weekends at Huby at the family's cottage young Polly Hebden could relax in loose frills (Plate 65) although she preferred more formal stripes and gaudy hats (Plate 66). As a 'new' young woman, she spent much of her leisure time on court or on wheels. That was in itself enough to earn her disfavour: 'Bicycling is far beyond a girl's strength. Not only that—it tends to destroy the sweet simplicity of her girlish nature. Besides, how dreadful it would be if by some accident she were to fall into the arms of a strange man.'[4] If a family anecdote is to be believed, it was in just such a fall that Polly Hebden landed in Alfred Atkinson's arms.

He, too, was a keen cyclist and had to ride in the face of criticism which persisted at least until the end of the century. Some thought the new fashion merely vulgar, while others hated the bicycle itself:

> It was but a strange, ingenious compound of dulness and danger. It kills some of its riders and bores the rest.... It was as inevitable as it is unlovely and I must put up with it.... It gratifies that instinct which is common to all stupid people, the instinct to potter with machinery.[5]

Alfred Atkinson, however, had also taken up another hobby universally approved as genteel. He had a camera and went with Polly Hebden's brother in search of good pictures. As a team they might have achieved great things but within twelve months William was dead. He complained of a 'sudden indisposition' and died of diphtheria.

Alfred Atkinson kept up his hobby. He took his camera to Huby and saw the Hebdens in their leisure (Plates 67 and 68). He captured Polly on plates and she in return caught his eye. As 'foreground interest' in Alfred's pictorial studies she was invaluable and long-suffering and must have lent enchantment to the view (Plate 69). Seven years after her brother's death, Polly and Alfred were married in Queen's Street Congregationalist chapel, Leeds, on 11 September 1895.[6] They set up home at 19 Carlton Mount.

Up to this point in the Atkinsons' story I was dependent on library records, family documents and the occasional good story. Once the family moved into the twentieth century, into their Edwardian heyday and beyond, there were living memories to draw on. One person, in fact, could go back, before the turn of the century, to Alfred and Polly in Carlton Mount: Mrs Ethel Simpson of Keighley, Yorkshire. She wrote saying she would be glad to talk.

My visit was a real occasion for her, now a widow of eighty-three with no family and few friends. She had 'bottomed' the house (i.e. spring-cleaned) and cooked specially for me. She needed no prompting and I sat almost silenced by an afternoon of resolute reminiscence. At the turn of the century she was a very young girl, so her memories were vague. In the end, however, a simple picture emerged.

Ethel Langham was born in 1894 and her family moved to Carlton Mount a few years later from Armley so that her father could be near his work. He was a chief cutter for Joseph Hepworth and suffered from chronic bronchitis. He rented number 9 Carlton Mount, while Alfred and Polly Atkinson owned their house at the other 'smart' end of the street with a big bay window and 'lovely furniture'. Soon the Langhams moved but only a few yards round the corner; they bought the end house of a terrace of six in Dorrington Road where Ethel lived in fear of a mad horse in the stables behind and where her father built a photographic darkroom up in the attic.

Mr Langham was a keen photographer but all that survives is a handful of family snaps: Ethel and her brother, Francis, outside 9 Carlton Mount; and, more exciting, Ethel and Francis with young Kathleen Atkinson outside the garden at the end of the street. Although she was six years her senior, Ethel was a playmate of Kathleen's and kept in touch for over sixty years until she was 'dropped' in Kathleen's confused decline at Huby.

The Langhams were welcomed and photographed at Huby (Plate 70) in the early days but they knew their place. When Mr Langham died, Alfred Atkinson bought up his house. He already owned the rest of the terrace and now he converted the whole lot into joinery works.

Ethel's memories of the Atkinsons and Carlton Mount were happy, in contrast to much of the rest of her life. Fortune's slings and arrows had left her scarred. Francis, her brother, who, in surviving pictures is clearly one on whom assurance sits, was, she claimed, a wastrel. He always came home late from work, too fond of 'looking at actresses' and he married a German girl with airs. She was happier spending money in Harrogate than running the sweet shop in Otley.

Mrs Simpson's memories of Alfred and Polly in Carlton Mount mark the point at which the Atkinson story becomes no longer simply history. Much of the rest of the story, though set in distant time, was still very much alive.

While Alfred and Polly were neighbours of the Langhams in Carlton Mount, the Atkinson children were born: Ethel in 1897 (but she lived only two months), Kathleen in 1899 and Christine in 1902. Inevitably, Alfred's camera now also became an adjunct to his family life and he recorded the growth of his daughters with the usual father's pride.

This album of sweets (Plates 71–5) has that strange ambivalence towards children which typifies the age, an age that saw children both as embodying innocence and prefiguring experience, as trailing clouds of glory but also fathering the man. In pictures the Atkinson girls are either little women in the trappings of old age or outsize dolls with flowers thrust into their grasp. Max Beerbohm, for one, in 1899, objected to having his sky darkened by such an over-indulged 'Cloud of Pinafores':

… If the nursery be turned into a free republic
and be rid of its old gloom and vigilant
authority, it must be the scene of absolute
happiness and its children, when the time
comes for them to leave it, will be appalled by
the serious side of life. Finding no pleasure in a
freedom they have always had, incapable of that
self-control which long discipline produces,
they will become neurotic, ineffectual men and
women.

The battle between liberals and repressives had, then, been fought long before Dr Spock. Mr and Mrs Atkinson spared the rod and opinions differ on the consequence to their children. Kathleen was a favourite, no doubt because the first-born lived only two months. In her parents' eyes Kathleen eclipsed the sun, which explains why, for every ten pictures of her, flounced and furbelowed, there is only one of her younger sister. Kathleen, frothing with lace, was exhibited to guests. Later, at Huby, fantastically got up, she was called on to perform her precocious routine, invariably the 'Persian' dance. Christine and any young friends who had suffered the spectacle before would grimace and exchange furtive asides: 'Oh Lord, Kathleen's going to dance again!' They would escape to the kitchen to play 'Snap' or 'Beggar My Neighbour' with young Annie, the maid. But this is to anticipate; until 1904 the Atkinsons were living in Carlton Mount.

When Alfred and Polly moved to Fir Tree House, it had been in the family for twenty years. It is ironic that, in a family whose wealth lay in property and which hoarded minutiae, the title deeds to the house should now be lost; but the family did preserve a record of its original purchase. Someone had a copy of an official notice of auction and scribbled on it the actual details of bids and purchasers. Later, as the notice began to disintegrate with age, the family backed it with linen. From the details one can reconstruct the sale.

In May 1883, Messrs Dacre and Son, auctioneers of Otley, offered seven lots by auction, 'splendid sites for the erection of houses', 'in the midst of a charming district', close to Weeton station on the North-Eastern Railway, nine miles north of Leeds. Mr Norfolk and Mr Mann, owners of the land, were offering an affluent few the chance to work among factories and live among fields. Lot five was the choicest, being more than mere grassland. Its official designation ran, 'The Dwelling House, with Barn, Cow House and Other Outbuildings, together with a close of grass known as Back Garth, containing 1a. 1r. 1p., pleasantly situate in the village of Huby'.

Bidding opened at 5 p.m. on Friday, 4 May, at the Royal White Horse Hotel, Otley. The early lots were knocked down quickly after brief exchanges. Mr Clapham bought six acres on Harrogate Road for £700; Mr Westerman bought the two acres of Long Close for £205. Predictably, lot five was hotly contested: the first bid was for £150, the second £155; the third, intended to clinch the matter and silence opposition, jumped to £200. But the others responded and in a series of strategic moves of £5, £10 and £15, the price climbed to £300, where 'this

inducement to purchasers seldom to be met with' was knocked down to Mr William Hebden of Leeds. After the excitement of lot five, the sale resumed a more perfunctory course.

For some reason the Hebdens kept their new property in Huby as a weekend and holiday retreat until 1899, when William retired. He only enjoyed a quiet life at Huby for another five years and, on his death, 5 March 1904, Fir Tree House, as it was now called, was valued for probate at £910. This was based on the estimated rent on the buildings and the value of the land if sold for building at 2s. per square yard. Polly Hebden (William's daughter and now Mrs Atkinson) and her husband were, however, less concerned with the material value of the house than with its magnificent potential. They abandoned plans for a house they were building for themselves at Menston, near Leeds, and moved in to live with Mrs Hebden (who lived until 1917). They considerably extended Fir Tree House—more than doubled its size, in fact. They installed a luxurious central-heating system (which lasted for seventy years). Here at Fir Tree House the Atkinsons lived in a style unabashed to the point of display (Plates 76 and 77).

One of those who held the centre of the stage at Fir Tree House is still alive—Christine, the younger daughter. She was born in 1902, two years before the Atkinsons moved to Huby. She later married Dr Linfoot of Otley and eventually moved south to Hampshire where she lives now, a widow. Godfrey Linfoot is her son.

I wrote to Christine Linfoot with some trepidation, since she might justly have objected to intrusion into her past. She was, however, glad that someone was showing interest in her father's pictures and invited me south to see her. Her present home was outwardly unassuming: a small bungalow on a modern estate. Inside there were a few reminders of life on a larger scale—a clock, a bureau, a chair—all looking uncomfortably overdressed in plainer surroundings. Mrs Linfoot was immediately recognisable as the girl in the pictures (Plate 78); in her face survived the character which is more than the sum of individual features. She soon dispelled any nostalgic preconceptions about her being frail: she still drove herself everywhere in her own car. And she had a sharp memory for detail: 'Most people would call it a summerhouse, but we used to call it the arbour.'

Mrs Linfoot named people and places, explained connections and relived occasions: the family picnic at Almscliff Crag (Plate 79); and the Dick Whittington pageant at Easter 1916, 'That's me on the left; I played the Queen' (Plate 80).

The mystery of one photograph was explained (Plate 81). It was taken, Mrs Linfoot said, in a railway carriage that stood at the top of the garden at Huby and was used as a summerhouse. In the picture Alfred Atkinson's family and friends look formally informal in the gloom. In trying to show little, their faces give away much. Although the photograph was taken about eight years before Mrs Linfoot was born, she could identify the sitters. The Reverend Hartley Waite, with gun and maniacal stare, was a family cousin; Tom Walsh, looking clean and humble like Mr Polly, was a decorator in Leeds; his serene wife, her hat a cross between fruit stall and entomological museum, went to school with Polly Hebden; the Walshes' daughter, Elaine, looks like a spectre; Polly Hebden herself perches like a sparrow, elegantly frilled; while William Hebden, her father, presents his best side with colonial assurance.

These photographs, however, amount to no more than minutes in an age. Life at Huby, Mrs Linfoot insisted, was generally boring for children. There was little to do and nowhere to go. Though we envisaged her life as golden, she thought it grey. What we had been too ready to romanticise and expected to be cause for nostalgia, she refreshingly painted with few tints of rose. Here was a life made up first of routine, with conflicts and crises, but in which there was enough money to be bored in comfort.

Father used to walk down to catch the train into Leeds each morning, the 8.16 from Weeton. Edgar Loveday started at 7.30. He was our gardener and Tom Wilson helped him. He had to walk three miles from Rigton; then Mother lent him her tricycle—solid tyres, you know. . . . Kathleen was sometimes spiteful; I remember she hid my comb and once she locked me in the loft where we kept the apples. She wasn't very interested in playing with the other children. She sometimes worked on the car with the chauffeur, decoking the engine. Father had two cars: he thought the big Armstrong was rather showy, so he bought another one for going round to see the men on the building sites. He would never drive himself. He didn't like walking either and we had to clean his shoes. He used to line them up in the kitchen for us. . . . We were never very close to Mother. If we had anything personal we used to tell the maid. . . . Mother used to wear a wig, you know—a 'transformation' they used to call it. She had her hair cut short and frizzed when she was young and never grew it long again. . . . Father was always doing something with photography; we had blinds in the bathroom and he developed plates there. We all helped in the printing; we laid out the negatives and paper in little frames in the sunshine on the lawn.

These memories of Mrs Linfoot's childhood at Huby brought back the sounds of those days as more than mere echoes; and the loudest was the polite clatter of knives and forks. Nothing so well expressed the Atkinsons' ability to enjoy themselves as the priority they gave to food. Not that their indulgence was immoral: organised gluttony was part of the Victorian and Edwardian canon:

Creatures of the inferior races eat and drink; only man dines. . . . Dining is the privilege of civilisation. The rank which people occupy in the grand scale may be measured by their way of taking their meals, as well as by their way of treating their women. . . . The nation which knows how to dine has learned the leading lesson of progress. It implies both the will and the skill to reduce to order, and surround with idealisms and graces, the more material conditions of human existence; and wherever that will and skill exist, life cannot be wholly ignoble.[7]

Though the new edition of Mrs Beeton's book, issued during or just after the First World War, omitted this particular passage, the principle was retained elsewhere: 'The moral and spiritual welfare of mankind depends largely on its breakfast.'

Alfred Atkinson was not lacking in moral stature in that respect. He had an extra-large dining table made at the joinery works for Fir Tree House. Full board at Huby was an accepted fact of life. Like Chaucer's Frankeleyn, Atkinson held that whole-hearted indulgence was 'verray felicitee parfit'. Lunch was central to his working day and much of his business was done over this protracted event. He was also a member of the 'Stepping Stones', a private dining circle which met regularly at Jacomelli's restaurant in Leeds. They feasted and flattered each other by turns on their birthdays and fêted Alfred Atkinson in 1935 as one who had 'changed the face' of the city.

It came as a surprise to me to learn that the Atkinsons had no motor car until after the First World War. The fact is that the motor car offered aspiring families an independent means of transport much cheaper than the carriage. At the turn of the century a small car could be run for about 4d. per mile, whereas even a pony trap might run to 6d. per mile—and that in the country. Alfred and Polly Atkinson were certainly not averse to the excitement of motoring (Plates 82–5). They refer to an 'adventurous' journey by car around Florence in 1913 and that is more than a wry comment on Italian drivers.

Alfred Atkinson, however, never drove himself on more than two wheels. Possession of a motor car, therefore, involved a secondary problem, neatly put by Alfred Harmsworth (later Lord Northcliffe):

A prime difficulty of the establishment of a motor car is the chauffeur or engineer. The perfect motor servant should be a combination of gentleman and engineer. He is the new type of man and will require the wages of other engineers. I do not think that a competent, well-mannered engineer will ever be obtainable for 30s. per week.[8]

However, the occasion produced the man— Battinson of Wetherby. He had learned his mechanics making motorbikes at Cleckheaton before enlisting as aircrew in the Royal Flying Corps. He was a gentleman's gentleman, adept with both rod and gun. He moved with his family into the cottage adjoining Fir Tree House as Alfred Atkinson negotiated the purchase of his first car.

It was a massive, 2.3-litre Armstrong-Siddeley '18', noted for its solidity and ease of driving more than for its zest (Plate 86). It certainly had style; Alfred saw to that by specifying extras. 'On the road' in January 1923, complete with 'nickel-plated radiator cowl' and 'gradient meter', WY 7032 cost precisely £899 4s. The second car, for business, was also an Armstrong, the '14', at about £400. Other cars followed in a magnificent cavalcade: two 30 h.p. Armstrongs, a Riley '9', a Bentley, a 20 h.p. Lagonda (Plate 87) and then, in 1931, by any standards, a 'special'. In November, 1931, the sales manager of the Central Garage, Bradford, wrote to Alfred Atkinson with advance details of the new 7-seater 'Selector' Lagonda with 3-litre engine, close-ratio gearbox and coach-built body. Someone has screwed up the letter as if to throw it away—perhaps Alfred himself at the first idea of such fantastic expense. But the garage knew well how to woo its customers. Enclosed with the letter they sent a blueprint of the machine and hand-painted artist's impression of the finished job. The cost? £1200, 'with everything of the very latest'. This was a car for the rich; those who had second thoughts could not afford it. Buying it was Alfred Atkinson's most flamboyant gesture.

The car was no mere showpiece, however; Alfred possibly justified the expense by reflecting how much of his family's time was spent on four wheels. Their first Armstrong Siddeley covered 25,000 miles before it was a year old. Battinson's recorded mileage in one later car log, for three months of 1930, reads: February, 1,562 miles; March, 1,080 miles; April, 2,358 miles. And two of these months are really low season. Battinson also recorded the names of no less than twenty-six hotels they stayed at in April, July and September of the same year. One tour alone reads: The White Lion, Banbury; The Crown, Blandford; The Victoria, Sidmouth; The Manor, Dousland; The Ship, Alveston; The Royal, Ross-on-Wye; The Raven, Shrewsbury; and one no less sumptuous but totally illegible at Holmbridge.

Once the Atkinsons owned a motor car, the Lake District, especially, became their second home. The Cumbrian Hills were to them what the 'Delectable Hills' were to Bunyan's Pilgrim, except that railways and roads had made the journey less perilous.

The opening-up of the lakes to middle-class

tourists in the nineteenth century had worried the natives. William Wordsworth, for example, was not happy about yielding up to the masses the country-side that had haunted him 'like a passion'. He contributed a sonnet to a pamphlet, 'On the projected Kendal and Windermere Railway' published in 1844:

> Is then no nook of English ground secure
> From rash assault? ...

But the invaders came. Many of them stayed and built their villas at Windermere. Ironically, it was partly Wordsworth's poetry itself which invited them; not just the great poetry but probably more the embarrassing verses of the long years of his poetic decline. Even the smallest stream was grist for the poetic mill and the sites honoured by impromptu sonnets and effusions were thus sanctified for later disciples. Wordsworth's verses appealed to pious Victorians; they lent their travel an air of moral purpose.

One such earnest traveller was Percy Lund, of Bradford, a photographer friend of Alfred Atkinson. He illustrated his travels in a lantern-slide lecture to a meeting of photographers which Atkinson also attended at Gloucester in 1899:

> Believing that to study the poems of
> Wordsworth in the midst of those rare natural
> surroundings which inspired them would at
> once be the best way of finding the truths they
> hold, and arriving at a full appreciation of the
> country we call Wordsworth's, I began not long
> ago, at those times which I could spare from a
> busy life, such a course of work ... seeking

> To look upon the hills with tenderness
> And make dear friendships with the streams and
> groves.

> The scheme was ambitious—an attempt to
> grasp the connection between nature, art and
> poetry...

Pretentious nonsense, perhaps, but that kind of sentimental reverence lent spice to Victorian life.

The prospects which appealed to them most were those amalgamations of limpid water and misty distances evoked by these Wordsworthian lines composed in 1834:

> Soft as a cloud is yon blue ridge—the mere
> Seems firm as solid crystal, breathless, clear
> And motionless; and, to the gazer's eye,
> Deeper than ocean, in the immensity
> Of its vague mountains and unreal sky.

The Atkinsons were creatures of similar sensibility and Alfred's pictures exude a tranquillity and easy pace more difficult for the casual tourist to find today (Plates 88–92).

The Atkinsons, however, gave due priority to their physical comforts. They usually stayed at The Swan, Newby Bridge, now a substantial place with thirty-six bedrooms and standing in seven acres of grounds. As a gourmet, Alfred Atkinson would have appreciated 'the most original and interesting à la carte menu for miles around'. The Atkinsons preferred the less strenuous views of the fells; they could relax on the riverside terrace on warm afternoons with the hills in the distance and another prospect in view—'traditional and substantial afternoon teas'. In his time at The Swan, Alfred observed through the lens the unobtrusive life of the locals like the *al factotum* nearby who served petrol to the growing tourist traffic, maintained his boat, repaired the bridge and in between jobs snatched a furtive nap (Plates 93–5).

One might be forgiven for thinking that the post-war years were for Alfred and Polly Atkinson a permanent vacation (Plate 96). In a decade of diaries Polly records the condition of the cars and the journeys they did in the kind of fastidious detail mothers normally reserve for their children. These soulless gazetteers suggest that the business of Polly's life, as well as its solace, was visiting and news. She measured her enjoyment in miles; she was a lady for whom to travel was in itself to have arrived.

Saturday shopping in Harrogate for new gloves or shoes could well be a prelude to a circuitous tour round picturesque places with good hotels *en route* for lunch, tea and dinner (Plate 97). It was not unknown to set out for Filey (fifty miles away) at 2.30 p.m. for a mid-week afternoon outing. The more ambitious Saturday tour would take in the Lake District (Plate 98), Dales and North Yorkshire Moors, while Polly avidly collected place-names as boys note the numbers of cars:

> We had a glorious day out, 203 miles—first we

went to Skipton, Gargrave, Settle, Buckhaw Brow. Straight on to Kendal, to Windermere, turned off to Patterdale, down Kirkstone Pass, to Ullswater Hotel—had lunch, rested two hours, then went on to Pooley Bridge, to Askam and High Street, turned left to Lowther Park. Went through the park on to the Shap Road through Shap village, about two miles on the road we turned off to Orton and over the moors, gathered some heather and found a skylark's nest with five eggs in it, to Tebay and on our way past Tebay station on to Sedbergh where we stayed for tea and rest. Then we went up Garsdale to Newby Head, Hawes, Bainbridge, Aysgarth, Wensley, Leyburn, Middleham, Masham, Tanfield on to Ripon, Harrogate and home—a delightful warm fine day.[9]

And so on, day after day, week after week.

Events of national importance passed Polly by. The great upheaval of May 1926 might as well never have happened except that *en route* to Dacre Banks for tea Polly and Alfred 'came and went on the bye-ways owing to the General Strike of the Men'.

I had hoped that Polly's diaries would give a more private view of Fir Tree House but the most intimate facts concern the vagaries of Jumbo, the dog, who brought dead hedgehogs into the lounge three times in a week (Plate 99).

When luxury travel was for the Atkinsons almost a daily routine, the word 'holiday' must be reserved for journeys abroad. The Atkinsons travelled abroad with other photographers at least five times: to Brussels, Amsterdam, Rouen (Plates 100 and 101), Bruges and St Malo. Alfred was certainly in Russia, too, in 1899, probably on business—in so far as business and pleasure were kept separate.

Alfred and Polly spent Easter in Switzerland in 1912. There they tackled considerable Alpine walks with an intrepidity and dress which suggest they might have been doing an afternoon's shopping (Plates 102–4). In this they were but creatures of their time.

In their disregard of the dangers of the Alps, the English had earned the reputation which elsewhere they acquired for braving the midday sun. In fact,

the English taught the Swiss and others to enjoy their own mountains. As early as 1840, Dr Arnold wrote: 'Switzerland is to England what Cumberland and Westmoreland are to Lancashire and Yorkshire, the general summer touring place.' Until the middle of the century, however, the mountains were only looked at from a distance. Murray's Guide for 1851 comments that many who were rash enough to climb Mont Blanc were of unsound mind. What lent the slopes sanity and respectability was the formation, in 1857, of the Alpine Club—decidedly an English institution.

The Atkinsons, however, were part of a second wave of tourists lured over to the Alps by the popularisers of foreign travel among the middle classes, notably Thomas Cook and, later, Henry Lunn. In 1905 he set up a travel organisation especially for members of the Free Churches and introduced them to the less temperate delights of winter sports.

Not everyone was happy, of course, to swing open the gates of the 'playground of Europe' to the less well-to-do. Some ex-patriot English regarded their foreign havens as private property. The most vociferous was Charles Lever (alias 'Cornelius O'Dowd') who claimed that the tourists arriving in Italy were part of a government scheme for disposing of convicts. But the hordes went, nevertheless, and the Atkinsons were among them.

Alfred and Polly chose Italy for a holiday in 1913 and, unable to find an advertised tour which covered enough ground, they asked George Lunn's Tours Ltd to produce, as the Americans say, a personalised itinerary—to include Genoa, Rome, Naples, Florence, Venice and Milan. Not surprisingly, eighteen days were not enough: 'We only had time to pass along the roads and, as it were, peep through the doorways. Six months would be more appropriate.' (This and other comments here come from notes to accompany a lantern-slide show which Christine Linfoot found tucked away in a drawer.) Alfred and Polly travelled with typically English distrust of foreign eating habits: 'We should have had breakfast at the station at Chambery, but instead they put a breakfast basket aboard the train. This contained eatables and so-called wine to drink. We handed it to the plate-layers in Turin, not caring to risk our digestive organs.' Nor, it seems, were the Atkinsons' stereotypes very different from our own. Alfred wrote of Signor Tani, the appointed Roman guide: 'This gentleman was one of our surprises. We expected a voluble guide with a conductor's hat and much exaggeration of manner. Instead, he simply said, "I shall meet you in the forum".' (Plate 105) It was not long before Alfred and Polly were wise to the tricks of the trade: 'At the railway station the porter takes your luggage, carries it off the platform and you pay; another porter takes charge and you pay for a further service. The next time you carry your own bags.' Again: 'We had to leave Florence by an early train, 6.30 a.m. This was rather too early for the chef at the Hotel Minerva, but the waiter got out of the difficulty by putting yesterday's rolls into the oven to make them new again.' One senses that, apart from Alfred's sensitive appreciation of the buildings they visited, the Atkinsons on their holidays abroad remained intransigently Anglo-Saxon.

From their foreign travels Alfred and Polly Atkinson took back to Huby memories and souvenirs to enliven their soirées. Alfred showed his lantern slides in the Methodist church hall. They brought the Mediterranean sun and the chill of the Alps within reach of villagers who had, perhaps, never been further than Leeds.

[1] Dr Heaton to the Leeds Philosophical and Literary Society in the early 1860s.

[2] Once again, there is a link with Leeds Town Hall. Brodrick's design had for the most part been rendered into stone by Samuel Atack, but he went bankrupt in 1857 before the job was finished. Work on the Town Hall was handed over to several other contractors, including David Nichols. His daughter, Annie Elizabeth Nichols, married Henry George Atkinson, whose later wealth as a builder's merchant was also founded on a business bought from his brother-in-law, Joseph Lister Nichols, for £200, borrowed from his father in 1883. By 1905, with premises in the Calls, stores at Warehouse Hill and a branch in Sheffield, Henry George Atkinson had gone international—importing Swedish laths into Hull and Garston and Canadian pine into Lancashire ports. Henry George did well for himself but is not renowned in the family for throwing his money around. There is an apocryphal story, doubtless family lore in many parts of Leeds, which, if not true, ought to be and at least expresses the man. They say that Henry George cautiously refused a request to sink money into penny bazaars run by a Mr Marks, who subsequently found Mr Spencer more co-operative. Instead, Henry George sank capital into what had been his father's business and which his two brothers at first and then Alfred alone managed for over forty years.

[3] *Sylvia's Home Journal*, 1877.

[4] *Ibid.*

[5] Max Beerbohm, 'Fashion and Her Bicycle', 1899.

[6] It came as no surprise to learn that the two families were 'chapel folk'. The link between self-help and religious dissent is easily understood. Dr Smiles himself preached this work ethic: 'Honourable industry travels the same road with duty; and Providence has linked both with happiness. The gods, says the poet, have placed labour and toil on the way leading to the Elysian fields.' Thoughts such as these explain how a Congregationalist minister could say to Charles Booth, with no irony intended, 'Ours is not the Church of the poor'.

[7] Mrs Isabel Beeton, *The Book of Household Management*, 1861.

[8] *Motors and Motor Driving*, 1902.

[9] 3 July 1926.

ELLEN ATKINSON (NÉE BACKHOUSE)

POLLY HEBDEN, EARLY 1890S

62   POLLY HEBDEN AND NELLIE WAITE, HER COUSIN, 1887;
PHOTOGRAPH BY WILLIAM HEBDEN

63   THE SAME; PHOTOGRAPH BY ALFRED ATKINSON

POLLY HEBDEN IN
ARNCLIFFE WOOD, NEAR
WHITBY, 1889

67

8

THE HEBDENS AT HUBY,
ABOUT 1890
(WILLIAM HEBDEN SEN.
WITH GUN, WILLIAM
THOMAS HEBDEN
OILING THE LAWNMOWER,
AND NELLIE WAITE)

69

'*As foreground interest she was invaluable and long-suffering*'

RUSWARP, NEAR WHITBY, ABOUT 1890

'The Langhams were welcomed and photographed at Huby'

ABOUT 1900
(ETHEL LANGHAM AND HER BROTHER,
FRANCIS, IN FRONT; THEIR PARENTS BEHIND
WITH MRS ATKINSON AND KATHLEEN)

'*This album of sweets*' KATHLEEN ATKINSON, 1900–1905

71

72

73

74

FIR TREE HOUSE, ABOUT 1910

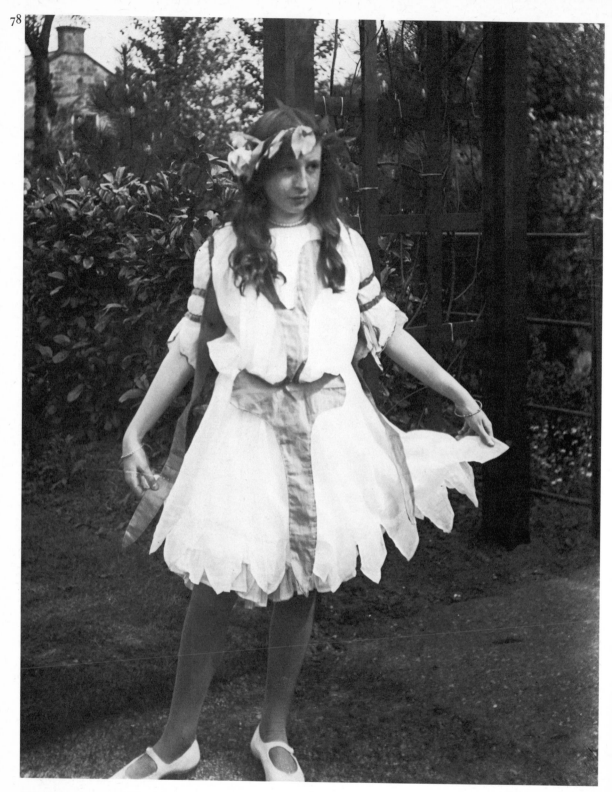

CHRISTINE ATKINSON, ABOUT 1914

'Father took the picture before we were ready'

9

ALMSCLIFF CRAG, ABOUT 1910

'I played the Queen'

DICK WHITTINGTON AT HUBY, EASTER 1916

*'Formally informal
in the gloom'*

81   THE RAILWAY CARRIAGE
       AT HUBY, ABOUT 1895

85

86

87 THE LAGONDA ON PICKERING MOORS, 1930

88 to 92

'Tranquillity and easy pace'

THE LAKE DISTRICT, 1897–1920

86 J. W. BATTINSON AND THE
ARMSTRONG-SIDDELEY, 1923

89

90

91

92

95

'A permanent vacation'

POLLY ATKINSON IN THE ROSE PERGOLA
AT HUBY, ABOUT 1925

*'Good hotels
en route'*

THE LAKE DISTRICT, 1930

97

THE LAKE DISTRICT, ABOUT 1920

'The vagaries of Jumbo'

100

ROUEN, 1925

I

102–4   SWITZERLAND, 1912

102

THE FORUM, ROME, 1913

4

DEVELOPMENT

ALTHOUGH CHRISTINE LINFOOT was the only survivor of the immediate family at Fir Tree House, I met several others who helped in the wings or merely observed the affluent pageant: relatives and friends, servants and villagers who looked up to the Atkinsons as *the* family in Huby. The memories of others helped present the Atkinsons more directly as people than as characters in a story. Those who knew the Atkinsons, however, were not simply sources of information; their own lives are, in a sense, also 'contained' in the pictures. Meeting them was, therefore, in itself a rich experience.

One of Mrs Linfoot's lifelong friends is her cousin, Phyllis Atkinson of Headingley, in Leeds. They were born within a week and have remained close for over seventy years. I called on Phyllis unannounced one summer weekend almost two years after I bought the negatives.

As a girl, Phyllis knew Alfred Atkinson as her 'posh uncle' — 'He always used to give us lovely Christmas presents'. She often took the train to Huby to play with her 'better-off' cousin. She remembers the gardener, Edgar Loveday, 'He used to give us rides in the wheelbarrow and we used to play croquet on the lawn'. Both Phyllis and Christine, however, found the atmosphere at Huby too stuffy and got away when they could to the freer air at Filey, where Phyllis's parents owned a cottage. In their teens the girls leaped at the chance to go away together to boarding school in Colwyn Bay.

That girlish delight in each other's presence has carried across to the present and gives them both an ingenuous vitality. One can see why Phyllis should be hurt when she overhears neighbours referring to the 'old lady' who lives in her house. She looked at the photographs that I showed her with an almost child-like delight: 'Ooh, that's Grandma!' (Plate 59). Later she recognised 'Grandfather Henry', too. She saw herself at Huby with Winnie, her sister, in

Japanese costume (Plate 106). And there were more playmates — Steven and Charlie Carr with their mother, Auntie Nellie, who lived next door but one (Plate 107). One casual group, whom no one had recognised, Phyllis immediately knew as Gilbert Whitaker's wife, Taira Mattiewich, and her children, Evald ('Chippy') and Mafelda, at Filey (Plate 108).

Phyllis told a bizarre tale of this branch of the family. Taira was the daughter of a well-to-do, possibly aristocratic, Russian family which lost almost everything in fleeing the Revolution. Taira's husband, Gilbert (one of Alfred Atkinson's nephews), had business which took him to India, where he died and the family vowed superstitiously never to visit the place again. Perhaps they remembered that Alfred Atkinson's uncle, Willie Chadwick of Whitby, had also died on his way to India [1] and sensed that for their family the whole continent was sinister. During the Second World War, however, Mafelda served as a nurse and, as luck would have it, was posted abroad. She did not return: the Japanese torpedoed the ship and Mafelda went down with the rest — in the Indian Ocean.

Phyllis Atkinson still lives in the house where she was born, one of a quiet terrace of six built by Atkinson and Sons in 1901. She still has the plans. The house is elusive and has a certain enigma. The road, which once bore the dignified name, Carriage Drive, is unmade and unadopted, a forgotten and secluded strip which it is easy to miss, even given directions. Oddly, the house is 19 Clarendon Road at the front and 29 Claremont Drive at the back. Isaac, Phyllis's father, complained to the authorities seventy-six years ago but their response has been slow. Meanwhile Phyllis helps baffled postmen by keeping her father's nameplate brightly polished on the gate. At the time the house was built, Isaac shared control of the family business with his brother, Alfred; but he died before he was fifty.

Phyllis has reason to remember the date: they buried her father on her tenth birthday.

Two months before Isaac's death, Phyllis's mother, knowing what was to be faced, took in a maid, in January 1912. Annie, then aged twenty, came on a month's trial; she stayed in service for the next sixty-one years until she died in 1973. In her last years, in a ironic reversal of roles, Annie was looked after by her mistress. A genuine survival from the world before the Great War, she never wanted or needed a life of her own, either its responsibility or its privileges.

Phyllis's house is now divided into two flats. She occupies the ground floor amid the styles of two ages—the graceless conversion of partition and breezeblock, and the ornamental plaster and mouldings of Edwardian times. One room remains much as it was then—the dining-room, now stripped of its huge oak table ('It fetched only half-a-crown in a sale twenty years ago'). But there still survives the monstrous tiled and mahogany fireplace, its overmantel set with mirrors and half-classical pictures. Carved in the mantel by one of the Atkinsons' craftsmen, is a tribute to Isaac's bluff domesticity: 'East, West; Home's Best'.

Other reminders of an earlier age, Phyllis nearly destroyed. In clearing out her father's safe in the attic twenty years ago to keep in it a silver tea service she had made herself, she came across several old books and papers. 'They weren't of any interest to me, though I had to laugh at the old prices. Everything was so cheap. I was going to throw them out but Cousin Fred said, "No, Phyllis, you keep them. Who knows, they might be of interest to someone some day".' So she wrapped them up in newspaper and put them in the cellar.

In that newspaper package in Phyllis Atkinson's cellar were the most exciting family documents I had yet seen. They brought to life Henry Atkinson's first years in the city of Leeds 125 years ago, before he set up the business. They confirmed the deductions that I had made in constructing the earliest years of the story and they pushed back the family origins by alluding to times tantalisingly just beyond reach.

The most precious survival is a pocket account book richly bound in (now soiled) white leather and held by a neat brass clasp. Today it would be used only for special inscriptions but Henry Atkinson assiduously recorded in it his daily expenses for several years from the summer of 1851. Here 'vermin killer', 'board and lodgings', 'ink-stand' and 'cherries' follow in incongruous sequence, their only link being that they lightened Henry's pocket. From the wealth of detail one can reconstruct the patterns of his life, his habits and tastes. Henry possibly bought such a smart book as a gesture of his determination to cope with his new independence away from home. When he inscribed the first page, he was a young joiner of twenty-eight lodged with Mrs Vince in Crossgates.

The book starts impressively with two journeys to London for a week at a time. Henry probably fixed his eyes on distant horizons and felt his fortune was to be made in the capital.[2] Even twelve months later, in 1852, now established in Leeds, earning twenty-four shillings for a six-day week (plus jobs 'on the side'—like making a mangle for Mrs Chadwick), Henry still had other ideas. He must have consulted his father (also called Henry) who wrote him a letter, the earliest surviving Atkinson document, penned by a surprisingly literate artisan hand:

My Dear Son, I Received Thy Letter on Sunday last and the Reason I have not writen before is thy Mother has been for coming to Leeds every day, we think that the Wages offered is too Small, I would not think of taking Less than thirty shillings, on any account, I think thou did quiet Right in Consulting Mr Chadwick on the Subjeck, also in referring them to him for both Carracter and ability also in referring them to Captain Ramsden for thy Family Carracter, but after all, I somehow think it will not be a Place that will suit thee and if it should not it will cost thee a deal of Money to get back again and so now my Son, you must consider the matter Well, Gentlemen are Such Changeable Creatures. Thy sisters hope they will not offer the thirty shillings and then they say it will keep thee at home, Mother and I returned from Methley by the half Past 2 o'clock Train and went from Leeds by the 4 o'clock Train Same day we found Grandfather rather better and we have not heard from him since we are all tolerably well at Present Thank God, I remain thy Affectionat Father, Henry Atkinson.

Either the thirty shillings were not forthcoming or Henry decided against entering a distant gentleman's service. His father's letter, grubby and creased from being kept in a pocket, Henry thought worth preserving. He may have seen it as a turning point in his life, when he dismissed his ambitions in London as a chimera, settling instead for a provincial and northern city.

In September, 1853, Henry Atkinson married Ellen Backhouse and put down roots in Leeds. That great event did not rate even a line in Henry's accounts but can be inferred from the 'complete inventory of sundry articles for furnishing my cottage' at 5 Carr Court—from Pembroke table (£1 5s.), rocking chair (13s.) and American clock (£1 8s.) down to mustard pot (1½d.).

Only one event is mentioned as such in the accounts—not Henry's marriage or the death of his father but, on 17 August 1853, 'Foundation Stone of Leeds Town Hall laid by John Hope Shaw, Mayor'. This confirmed the feeling that the building of the new Town Hall had an almost symbolic importance for the Atkinson family. Equally, Henry's place in the world of self-help became historical fact in the light of an account-book entry dated 24 May 1852, six weeks after Henry's arrival in Leeds: 'Entered Mechanics Institution, 7s.'. The Institute had been founded thirty years before to teach young working men the new science and technology.

Henry Atkinson's leisure included concerts at the 'Academy of Arts' and 'Bands on the Moor'. He also played music himself: 'February 4th, 1852, Music "Dead Leaves", 2s.; March 26th, 1854, Fiddle Strings, 4d.'. Other more personal touches are Henry's regular subscriptions to *Eliza Cook's Journal* and his unshakeable faith in 'Old Parr's Pills' at 1s. 1½d. per box.

Each detailed entry is a clue in another detective trail; the whole book is a catalogue of suggestive mysteries: 1 January 1852, 'At Leeds Seeing Monsieur Franconi's "Cirque de France", 2s. 7d.'; 20 April, 'Panorama etc, 1s. 3d.'; 12 July, 'Camera Obscura, 9½d.'; 23 February 1854, 'Supper at Hindle's Eating House for the whole shop, 2s. 8d.'; 15 January 1856, 'Paid fine for brother John, 6d.' (five days after the death of their father).

The second half of Henry's account book is given over to business and here the foundations of the family firm are laid bare. Henry's first self-employed venture was in partnership with brother John at the beginning of 1856. They borrowed fifty pounds from their father (five days before he died) and another fifty pounds from their mother two months later in March. Some of the money went to buy land—from David Hewson Waldby, who also supplied Henry and John with building materials. Within three years, however, the brothers had split up and Henry joined Waldby, where my account of the family's burgeoning originally began. Since Henry was living in Carlton Cross Street from 1856, it is likely that on the morning of Tuesday, 7 September 1858, he at least walked the fifty yards down Carlton Hill to see the Queen pass on her way to the Town Hall.

One relic in Phyllis Atkinson's cellar posed a challenge. It was an indenture dated 5 February 1781, between Addiman Barker, then a boy of twelve, of Penwell, Yorkshire, and Edward Middlebrough, wheelwright and carpenter of Aberford, near Leeds. The young lad was thus bound as apprentice for the next nine years. The actual terms of the agreement make the word 'apprenticeship' euphemistic for legalised slavery, since Addiman seemed to sign away most sources of pleasure, if not freedom. His parents even agreed to provide the yarn for his stockings. Now why should this agreement to which no Atkinson was party appear among Henry's effects? The family may have been hoarders for generations but none of the survivals have I had to dismiss as irrelevant curiosity.

Here was a problem of family trees, insuperable without possibly months of patient research. I never foresaw myself answering these questions, however, since they lay on the fringe of my real interest. At least it seemed appropriate that the search backward into the family origins should end on a puzzle.

There are times, however, when the course of this story has turned on uncanny coincidence. Some time after I had met Phyllis Atkinson, Alfred Atkinson's great-grand-nephew wrote to me. Jonathan Atkinson was direct descendant of Henry George Atkinson, Alfred's brother, who has an important niche in the story so far. Like his great-grandfather, Jonathan Atkinson had married into the Lister-Nichols family and preserved the link with Leeds Town Hall. Jonathan said his special interest was his family ancestors.

Though by now I had grown accustomed to good fortune, I could not, even at my most expectant, have foreseen such a stroke of luck. I drove to see Jonathan in Burley-in-Wharfedale wondering whether Addiman Barker would appear among the branches of the family tree.

Jonathan Atkinson professed to live in a menagerie of dogs, cats, hamsters (and goats next door). There is a tale in that, he said, as there is in the most ordinary things to do with his family. As a boy, he had been excited by the family folk-lore of shadowy great-grand-people and cousins with unquestioned existence but uncertain pedigree. From casual allusions he drew up a more rigorous inventory of family names, reaching back to the middle of the nineteenth century, to Henry Atkinson of Aberford.

To go back further required years of careful scrutiny of public and parish records but studying Theology at Oxford had taught Jonathan the virtue of patience. He used sources I was quite unaware of, such as Hearth Tax and Manorial Court records. The final compendium of dates, names and occasional trades, of Atkinsons variously spelled and with improbable Christian names—like Mungo or Wiral—was any telephonist's nightmare but a genealogist's dream. To put them together was like assembling a jig-saw in which half the pieces belong to a quite different puzzle. That challenge appeals to a special kind of mind such as that which delights in crosswords with unnumbered clues.

The result of Jonathan's dedication is a family tree of bewildering detail but very clear structure.[3] The Atkinson line goes back to the seventeenth century in Sandal, near Wakefield, where the destruction of records during the Civil War prevents further search. For several later generations the Atkinsons were artisans at Methley, near Wakefield. There Alfred Atkinson's great-grandfather lived. Alfred's grandfather moved to Aberford and his father to Leeds—where my story begins.

The mystery of Addiman Barker was easily solved: Alfred's grandfather, Henry (who wrote the letter quoted earlier), married Mary Barker, Addiman's daughter.

Some who served, or whose parents had served at Fir Tree House, wrote to me. The daughter of Edgar Loveday, the gardener, had several pictures, a canteen of cutlery—present to her father in 1917—and a trowel engraved, 'Huby Wesleyan School Stonelaying, 20th June, 1914'. One lady's mother had been Mrs Hebden's maid from 1887 to 1910 but she died some time ago. Her successor at Huby, however, Charlotte Annie Carrington (née Swift), was still alive, aged eighty-three, and lived at Rothwell, near Leeds.

I went to see her in her old people's flat. On the wall hung a prized reminder—a delicate watercolour of a woodland path painted by Kathleen Atkinson. Mrs Carrington said she entered service at Fir Tree House in 1914 at the age of nineteen. Actually, she had already been in Huby for a few years as maid to a family with more style than substance. If she had been out for the evening, her employers would insist that she put on her uniform again before serving the bedtime drinks. For this family service also had to be in part its own reward; so Mrs Atkinson had no difficulty in luring her to cross the village street for seven shillings per week, plus board.

Annie—as everyone called her—lived 'below stairs' at Fir Tree House for the next six years; metaphorically, that is, since her employers 'tret' her as an equal, provided she did her work. The Atkinsons obviously did not subscribe to the opinions of earlier severer employers: 'I really believe servants are only happy if their rooms are allowed in some measure to resemble the home of their youth, and not to be merely places where they lie down to sleep as heavily as they can.'[4] Annie had a 'nice little room' in Fir Tree House and ate the same food as the family. She had butter on her bread, unlike other servants in the village who, she said, only had margarine.

There were frequent parties, too, at Fir Tree House and, when the governess left, the former schoolroom was redecorated with a floor laid for dancing. There was a new phonograph with an enormous horn. Everyone wore evening dress, which made Annie feel shy, although she was invited to join in. Mrs Atkinson would say, 'Now then, who's going to fetch Annie and dance with her?' And the blushing girl would be importuned by gallants. Annie went more readily with Christine and Kathleen to dances at Weeton Institute and once went with them on holiday to Grange-over-Sands, actually sharing a bedroom.

Living in comfort gave Annie reason for guilt. While her parents struggled in a poor part of Leeds during the First World War, the Atkinsons lived in luxury. They often had more than they could eat. There was always fowl at weekends—pheasant and ptarmigan on Saturday, turkey and goose on Sunday.

On seven shillings a week Annie could not afford to travel home on her half-day, alternate Saturday and Sunday evenings; but, when she went home on her monthly day off, she always had flowers and vegetables from the garden for her family. Her father bred canaries and Annie took one back to Huby as a present for Kathleen. It used to raid the table for scraps of food in the course of a meal but no one seemed offended.

Annie herself observed the niceties of etiquette. Her daily routine started at 6.30 a.m., brushing the red drawing-room carpet before breakfast. House-cleaning, in fact, was her main chore. Two afternoons she spent on the silver; some of that had been brought from Russia by Taira Mattiewich's fugitive family. Kitchen work Annie shared with the cook. Monday was washday, using the huge tub in the back kitchen, where there was a well. The ironing had to be finished the same day, even if it meant staying up until one o'clock in the morning.

Mrs Hebden, Polly Atkinson's mother, no longer mistress in her own house, was a tyrant to please. Her bedtime milk was always too hot or too cold and she complained that her room (furnished in black oak) was always left dusty. In her last years, before 1917, she was even harder to live with. Annie said she 'went funny in her mind' and all the doors had to be fitted with chains to prevent Mrs Hebden wandering and waking the rest in the middle of the night with instructions to get up.

Annie's help, the cook, left in 1917 and went to join Lloyd George's 'canaries' in munitions. Thereafter Mrs Atkinson herself helped in the kitchen.[5]

The Atkinsons lost their gardener, too. Edgar Loveday went to fight and did not return after the War. The governess also went off to get married. Kathleen's schooling then stopped but Christine was sent for two years to Penrhôs Boarding School in Colwyn Bay.

Annie Swift's last two years at Huby were, then, quieter, even sad ones. The sense of Fir Tree House as a self-contained community had gone. Annie left in 1920 to look after her father who was ill. When she married in 1928, Mr and Mrs Atkinson drove over to see her and gave her a clock and an old suit for her father (it turned out to be too small). After Mrs Atkinson's death, Alfred came to see Annie again with a few keepsakes from his wife's effects. Although Annie was never paid much in service— only twelve shillings in 1920 (Mrs Atkinson claimed she could not afford any more!)—she considers the life she shared with the family at Fir Tree House was itself worth a lot more than wages. Strangely, Annie did not remember Alfred Atkinson as a photographer at all; nor does she appear in any of his pictures.

Two people at Huby, seen by everyone there as village 'elders', were often deferred to on questions of the past. I went to see them and found they both had some contact with Fir Tree House.

Mrs Jessie Hampstead, at eighty-six, was the oldest woman in Huby. She was horrified that young people—that is, those around sixty—should be so regularly struck down by disease and disaster. She attributed her own longevity to a life of hard work and boasted that there was not a house in the village that she had not scrubbed on her knees. She came from a family of twelve children. Her brother had cleaned the Atkinsons' shoes and Jessie used to wish that she might have shoes like theirs when she earned her own living. For about a year, around 1905, she had cleaned Fir Tree House when the Atkinsons were short of domestic help. Jessie remembered Mr Atkinson as a 'real gentleman' and his wife as bald, with a head 'like a plate of lard'.

'Old' Mr King had lived in Huby all his life. He knew and had known everyone in the village since he was born at the turn of the century on the family farm, now the Old Post-House. In those early days it had provided the Atkinsons with butter and milk. Later in 1920, the Kings had run the village store, where 'young' Mr King still lived. His father lived with an entourage of cats in a bungalow almost smothered by an unkempt front garden. He was so happy to talk about the past that he left his laundry draped around the lawn on a broken washing-line. As village shopkeeper, Mr King had inevitably been the privileged centre of several networks, though his direct contact with the Atkinson family had been rare since they ordered their groceries in bulk two months at a time from provision merchants in Leeds. Mr King helped them eke out if they ran short before the next order was due. He had also been called on as haulier to cart building materials for Mr Atkinson's local projects. A photograph of a thatched cottage which I could not identify (thatch is almost unknown in Yorkshire) reminded Mr King of a cottage in Huby, demolished before the First World War. He said he had transported the stones to the new Sunday School which Atkinson and Sons built in the village.

I discovered that one of Kathleen Atkinson's close friends, Alice Armitage, now lived in a Harrogate hospital where frailty confined her. Although her physical senses were blunted, her mind's eye was still sharp. She recited her memories, clear and precise, without context and sequence, like an album of mixed pictures.

Alice said she had first met the Atkinson sisters at a friend's house in Headingley, in Leeds. She remembered tea-parties in the gardens at Huby, held to raise funds for the institute. Sixpence was the standard charge for these events, known as Mrs Shaw's 'Knockouts' or Mrs Atkinson's 'Come All Ye's'. On one such occasion, when the family's hands were full, the eccentric Mrs Hebden, normally kept secure in her room with a hasp on the door, escaped. She seized her umbrella and set off down the road for the station. There she boarded the first train and was found some time later, lost and wandering in Northallerton. Poor John Lee, the porter at Weeton Station, pressed to explain why he let her go, could only plead, 'No one stops Mrs Hebden'.

Alice spent whole days, even weeks at Huby and, on occasions, when Mr Atkinson sent Battinson, the chauffeur, home from Leeds at lunchtime, Mrs Atkinson would improvise a festive expedition for her daughters and their friends. 'Come on, everybody, we've got the car! Where shall we go?' And they would pile into the Armstrong and set off for the Dales or the North Yorkshire Moors. There Alice would take photographs on her quarter-plate camera. She insisted that she did not look to Mr Atkinson for help; she developed her own plates at home in an improvised darkroom in the cupboard under the stairs.

Some of the memories of those I met added colour to the picture of life at Fir Tree House. Alfred and Polly, however, remained vague figures; very few seemed to have penetrated their guard. Despite their extrovert lifestyle, they were private people. Those who could remember them talked mainly about externals, although there is nothing unusual in that. We all sometimes measure out the lives of others in coffee spoons or wealth. That seems less unfair to the Atkinsons, however, than to many others. The family is defined best at their ease in Huby or travelling the country in search of diversion.

[1] When Willie Chadwick died, his widow, Anne, wrote to Alfred Atkinson with a faith which is moving and simple: 'Willie died twenty-four days after he left Cardiff and was buried in the Indian Ocean in a nameless grave, but the Master knows where it is and will call him up at the appointed time.'

[2] While he was in London, Henry Atkinson would certainly have been one of the six million visitors to The Great Exhibition in the new Crystal Palace.

[3] Mrs J. E. Panton, *From Kitchen to Garrett*, 1890.

[4] See edited version in Appendices.

[5] The War, in fact, destroyed the institution of domestic service. Girls used to regular hours, free evenings and good wages, even those who had worked in munitions, wearing oppressive respirators and grease on the face and exposed to toxic jaundice, were reluctant after the War to forfeit their independence by going back into service. As early as 8 December 1915, *The Times* predicted that 'the domestic servant will soon be as rare as breakfast bacon in Germany'.

5

THE CONVENTION

ONE WEEK EACH summer for over thirty years Alfred and Polly Atkinson travelled with other members of the Photographic Convention of the United Kingdom. I first came across this lofty title when I met Godfrey Linfoot. He had found at Fir Tree House, in a small black box lined with blue velvet, a silver presidential medal of the convention, dated 1923. It was the first and only intimation that Alfred Atkinson's photographs were not completely unknown outside the family. A convention as august as that, of course, had to have records; so I decided to restore the shine to Alfred Atkinson's medal of office. The research brought into focus, in detail I had not expected, the world seen through the lens almost a century ago.

My sources were standard: the *Amateur Photographer* and the *British Journal of Photography*. These are still published today, catering between them for most photographic 'buffs', not only those who take pictures but also those who merely talk cameras. The first issues of these two magazines, however, date from the earliest days of photography, 1863 and 1853. They now mostly collect dust in public libraries' hidden stacks, bound into tomes and given the rank of encyclopaedias. In the case of the Photographic Convention of the United Kingdom this posthumous status seems to have vindicated the high opinion it held of itself.

The convention's beginnings lay in a letter written to the *British Journal of Photography* on 22 January 1886, by Mr Andrew Pringle. He proposed an annual convention or congress of not more than a week in the summer months for amateur and professional photographers alike.

The date, 1886, is important. It was nearly half a century since the French painter, Paul Delaroche, on seeing the first Daguerrotypes in the summer of 1839, made his portentous claim for the camera: 'From today painting is dead'. Cameras had not, however, made brushes redundant; nor had they, before the 1880s, been in the hands of more than the truly dedicated. The early photographer needed not only camera and plates but also a portable darkroom in which to coat the glass plates with wet collodion immediately before exposure and to develop them immediately after. The camera could not be a casual adjunct to an afternoon stroll; to preserve fleeting moments the early photographer had to prolong them half-an-hour or more.

In 1871, however, Dr Richard Leach Maddox did for the camera what the transistor did for the radio. His invention of the 'dry' plate, which the photographer could carry ready coated with emulsion and take home to develop, put cameras within most people's grasp. This was not yet, of course, the age of the snapshot. Purists, in fact, preferred to use large glass negatives (even wet plates in the studio) until well into this century. In late Victorian times a stand camera, tripod and a dozen or more plates were cumbersome and heavy (Plate 109). Frank Sutcliffe, who can have been no sluggard, once timed himself unpacking and setting up his camera—one and three-quarter minutes, and that before focusing and inserting the slide. There was also what Sutcliffe called a 'glorious uncertainty' about exposure and development: the response to light of different batches of plates varied so much that successful exposure could be no more than inspired guesswork. Exposures of many seconds were common and exposures of several minutes were not unknown—even after the work of John Burgess, Richard Kennett and Charles Bennett in speeding-up the gelatine silver bromide used on the dry plate. Nevertheless, by 1878 four British firms were mass producing dry plates and the prophets of photography had a zealous host of new disciples.

Mr Andrew Pringle's idea of a yearly open convention, therefore, met with loud support. It was taken up in a *British Journal of Photography* editorial of 12 March 1886, and on 9 July details of the first, three-day convention at Derby were announced.

Forty-six members attended and heard an inaugural paper by H. P. Robinson, one of the Establishment figures in Victorian photography. He could not actually be present at Derby in person 'having been rescued from the portals of death by a severe surgical operation, from the effects of which he was only slowly recovering'. But he wished the convention success, quoted Byron to little purpose and relegated Socialism 'to the congenial street mud in which it usually wallows'. He was preaching to the converted: the Photographic Convention was, if nothing else, a social elite.

They did Robinson the honour of inviting him to be their President in 1891. He declined, since a speech impediment would prevent his reading a presidential address. The convention, however, shouted louder and prevailed on him in 1896 when the meeting came to the Queen's Hotel, Leeds.

That year was remarkable in several respects. In addition to the usual lectures, excursions, garden party and civic reception, Robinson, as President, established what was to be an important annual event: the exhibition. He selected prints made by famous names—Sutcliffe, Davison, Hollyer, Burchett (and himself!). All had hung at the Salon in London. Included at Leeds was Frank Sutcliffe's most famous picture, 'Water Rats', and he appeared at the convention for the first time to read a paper.

In his talk, 'Photography at the Seaside', Sutcliffe bewailed the loss of Whitby's status as a port and spoke ironically of his too-many imitators—like the stranger who was 'waiting on the bridge for a boatload of naked boys, but could not make out why they were so long'. Nevertheless, Sutcliffe invited all 300 convention members to take their cameras to the coast and point them at the nice people there.

> Not the least picturesque part of the seaside are the inhabitants thereof, especially the fishermen. Their distinctive dress of sou'ester, guernsey and seaboots would be worth taking alone; but when you have besides a handsome, open face, absolutely without guile or deceit of any kind, the photographer and not the model will be at fault if the photograph turns out a failure.

One member of Sutcliffe's audience, at least, was attending the convention for the first time—Alfred Atkinson then of Carlton Hill (Plate 110). He was destined to be President himself twenty-seven years later. Actually, he did not need Sutcliffe's invitation to visit Whitby: he had family there, an uncle and aunt, Willie and Anne Chadwick, of St Hilda's Terrace, whose children, like most others in Whitby, sat for their carte-de-visite portraits in Frank Sutcliffe's studio. Alfred had known Whitby, then, since he was a boy. He took pictures of it as soon as he had a camera (Plate 111) and he took his family on holiday there until the First World War. One of his photographs (Plate 112) is directly inspired by one of Frank Sutcliffe's most copied pictures, nicknamed, 'Stern Realities'.

In many ways the Photographic Convention of the United Kingdom was old-fashioned. It is significant that its champion in the early years was H.P. Robinson who set himself against the newfangled 'Impressionists'. The convention, of course, did embrace all shades of opinion: the 'Impressionist', P.H. Emerson, himself led a convention excursion to Oulton Broad in 1897 when they met at Great Yarmouth. In general, however, the conventioners loved recognised haunts and picturesque views. In this they were not unlike those eighteenth-century travellers who set out equipped with 'Claude glass' to view 'picturesque' Nature reduced to a two-dimensional handful. For many conventioners the camera's viewfinder acted as a 'Claude glass' with the added advantage of offering a permanent record in the form of a negative.

The road to a good picture, then, was a country road (Plates 113-7), not the city streets, as the *B.J.P.* constantly reminded the convention: 'There is not much of photographic interest in the city of Leeds. Although there are numerous good buildings in the city, probably the Town Hall is the only one that will have any attraction for the members of the convention.'[1] They focused instead on abbeys and castles. Other recommended sites during their week in Leeds were Adel church (Plate 118)—'the old Norman arch is considered by archaeologists to be the finest in the country'—and Roundhay Park—'beautifully situated, it is very extensive but contains only a few features of interest to the photographer' (Plate 21).

The conventioners, however, took both pictures and tea. And they feasted their stomachs even more than their eyes (Plate 119). Their dinners were lavish. The Mayor of Ludlow served up this lunch for the convention in the Town Hall on 19 July 1895: clear soup; mayonnaise of salmon and cucumber, soles in aspic, mayonnaise of lobster, plain lobster, dressed crab, braised tongue, boiled chickens, roast chickens, spiced beef, roast ribs of beef, roast lamb with salads, lamb cutlets in aspic, pigeon pies, veal and ham pies; fruit pies, fruit, cheese and butter; champagne, claret, whisky, ale, lemonade and soda water. For this the members paid 5s. 6d. A decade later entertainment was included at the same price:

> Colonel Plunkett gave the toast of 'The Ladies' which was responded to by Mrs Catherine Weed-Ward. During the evening many excellent musical entertainments were given. Mr Clark Berry's band supplied a programme of music during the dinner, and after the dinner Mr Gerald Ewing and Mr Fred Jeffs contributed notably to the enjoyment of the company by some excellent songs. The latter also amused his hearers very much as a raconteur. The remarkable sleight-of-hand performances of Mr W.F. Cooper, 'Presto', further diversified the entertainment very agreeably.[2]

Possibly the central event of the convention's week, even more prestigious than the civic reception, was the President's 'at home'. Once, at Southampton in 1906, the convention was entertained (all at once?) on the President's yacht, although, more usually, they kept their feet on the ground with a garden party (Plate 120)—complete with frills.

Those who attended the second Derby convention in 1904 were fêted in style. That year the President was a local J.P., appropriately named Herbert Strutt, who lived at Bridgehill, Belper. On the Wednesday afternoon, 13 July, over three hundred conventioners met at Derby station and, doubtless to the dismay of other travellers, jostled *en masse* onto the 2.15 train. A few more affluent and much more courageous motored over to Belper. As the cars rattled north through the villages that flank the A6, scattering stones and unwary pedestrians, their occupants dressed in capes and goggles, the locals

must have thought that the horsemen of the Apocalypse had taken to wheels. However, the motorists alighted intact on the drive at Bridgehill and Mr and Mrs Strutt received all the guests in the house.

The host had reason to reflect, with an eye to his pocket, that at the first Derby convention, eighteen years before, there were only forty-six members to entertain. Mr and Mrs Strutt catered for over three hundred. For weeks local photographers who weren't members of the convention had cast nervous eyes over their morning post for an invitation to 'The Event'. It fell to the Strutts to decide who was anyone in photographic circles around Derby.

The afternoon of the garden party was glorious July sunshine or, as they used to say in the reports, 'the clerk of the weather was kind'. The sun made the two large marquees on the upper and lower lawns at Bridgehill as necessary as if it had been raining. To bask and go red in the sun was still decidedly unfashionable. At least the sun allowed the Strutts to lay Persian carpets and rugs on the grass.

In the tents were the refreshments. Tea and coffee, sherry and claret cup, cake and biscuits were regarded as 'indispensable' in respectable circles. The Strutts provided more than the bare minimum to preserve their reputation. After all, it was strawberry time and there were accordingly fruit and ices in the upper tent. Mrs Stone of the County Hotel, Derby, was in charge of the catering. Her days of hard work earned her the accolade of 'satisfactory' in the *B.J.P.* Such faint praise damns her; something was decidedly not right.

As was the fashion, a military band was engaged to play at the party from four o'clock on. Under Bandmaster Seddon the First VB Sherwood Foresters played an album of lollipops, including, 'The Merry Monarch Overture' (Hérold), 'A Life on the Ocean, Fantasia' (Miller) and a negro dance, 'Sambo's Holiday' (Tchakoff). Quite properly, the whole party stood silently to attention on the lawns and terraces as 'God Save the King' brought to a close 'an exceedingly delightful afternoon'.

Travellers coming south from Sheffield by express train in the late afternoon were somewhat surprised by an unscheduled stop at Belper station. Poking inquisitive faces out of the windows, they were amazed to see a fashionable throng on the platform, taking farewell snaps, like massed guests from a wedding, and then, for the second time that day, invading the train. In those days the Convention Garden Party was an event of some moment; even the railways stopped their trains especially for them.

There were some, if not many, who felt ill-at-ease in this 'Picnic Convention', among the Strutts and the Plunketts, the names themselves redolent of leisurely times. There seems to have been a clash in the convention between the divergent interests of those to whom 'plates' suggested cameras and those for whom they promised food. Thomas Bedding, convention President in 1900 and editor of the *B.J.P.*, published his 'diary' as a sardonic comment on the mixed diet of zealous pseudo-science and elegant promenading:

Friday. Excursion. Attempt to 'do' the third largest county in England in eight hours. Discussions *en route*: colour photography, stereography and benzole derivatives. Am asked to give formula for best developer. Reply: H2o = hydroxyl-mono-hydride, q.s., qualified according to taste and circumstances. Photograph Norman arch with crowd looking on. Shutter sticks. Crowd sniggers. Told camera wasn't level; that it had moved; that I had over-exposed, under-exposed and not exposed at all. Smile benignly. Lunch. More speeches. Tell a story—for the first time not about a parrot and a dog. Everybody delighted and shaked hands with me. Castle of Five Acres! Not big enough. Still chided for getting in the way of conventioners giving ten-minute exposures to one-second subjects. Homeward journey devoted to taking photographs of the president. Novel experience. Start dinner at 7.45, finish at 7.59. Papers and slides 8.00 to 10.30. Discussion on things in general. 12.30 to bed. Woke up at 2.30 by a conventioner anxious to tell me the latest good story. Saved him the trouble as politely as I could. Made an enemy of him.[3]

Most difficult was to satisfy all members in the choice of papers to be read. Any one convention,

Southampton for example, might be addressed on both 'The Differentiation of Bacillus, Coli Communis and Bacillus Typhoons by means of the photographic plate' (W.C. Stevenson) and, 'Old-English Manners and Customs' (Sir Benjamin Stone). If anything, the holiday-makers won the day over the boffins, so that 'Cosmos' (of the *B.J.P.*) could report on 15 July 1898: 'There were top hats for the first time in the convention history. I wonder if, after all, the appearance of those highly-polished cylinders is to be interpreted as an indication that the convention is on the way to becoming an institution for Superior Persons!'

Dwindling and reluctant audiences eventually killed the learned paper at convention meetings. The *Amateur Photographer* marked its passing, at Scarborough, with an obituary notice:

The conventioners seemed determined to give themselves up to Yorkshire revelry, and technical matters are not only relegated to the tail-end, but to the endmost hair of the tail. The papers read at the convention in recent years have furnished an excellent study in the art of growing beautifully less. I am old enough, speaking conventionally, to remember when they even wrangled over the speeds of plates, while the July sunshine tempted them in vain. This year there is no paper at all.[4]

That tone is regret; but five years earlier the editor of the *Amateur Photographer* had put the issue much more frankly:

How far a number of excursionists intent upon nothing more important than a week's sightseeing at co-operative prices are justified in calling themselves the Photographic Convention of the United Kingdom is a question which some day may have to be answered, for no one can at the moment pretend that the convention does any good to photography ... for any one name of any importance which will be found on the list ... one might mention fifty leaders in photography, men of real influence and importance, who have never taken part in this preposterous picnic party.

Even the unofficial good times at the convention

unashamedly reached print: an anonymous chick reported the fun to be had 'when the cock and hen brigade were gone to bed'. One young man, wanting to join an after-hours seance at Southampton, had to climb through the hotel window, 'admission through the front door being denied by the hotel Cerberus'.[6]

The list of convention venues from 1895 onwards reads like a recommended tour of the fashionable resorts and watering places of the United Kingdom. They include Oxford and Cambridge (Plates 121 and 122), Bath (Plates 123 and 124)[7] and Scarborough, Hereford (125 and 126) and Gloucester (127 and 128). Here the convention assembled, took over the towns and made themselves known in the countryside on daily excursions (Plate 129). Many small villages soon learned the art of posing for pictures, happy to acquiesce in the insurgents' terms:

To-day in the village, if anyone chooses to go, he will find Sarah Jane positively leap for the famous old bucket and carry it down the slope with the greatest unconsciousness and self-possession in the world. And he will find Giles hold his pitchfork a trifle more picturesquely, but otherwise never let it be known that he sees a camera within a thousand miles of him. And he will find granny smooth her frill and settle herself in the doorway as to the manner born.[8]

On Thursday, 13 July 1899, while the convention was at Gloucester, the village of Tintern on the banks of the Wye suffered her violation at the hands excursionists. Happily, history had taught her what to expect: she had been a well-established prospect in the picturesque tours of the eighteenth century, though not all admirers found her beauty without taint. William Gilpin (in *Observations on the River Wye*, 1782) felt that the gable ends of the famous abbey could be improved for tourists with an eye for ruins by taking a mallet to them. Fortunately, the abbey survived—though there was scaffolding there on the convention's visit (Plate 130).

For the Victorians, of course, Wordsworth's sense 'Of something far more deeply interfused' had thrown over Tintern that kind of religiosity which especially appeals to pious natures. The visit of the Photographic Convention in 1898, however, was for 'coarser pleasures': 'A vast array of photographic apparatus was lugged and tugged and hugged by a perspiring multitude of enthusiastic ladies and gentlemen in variegated costumes to the railway station *en route* for the Chepstow and Tintern excursion'.[9] Alfred and Polly Atkinson were of the party.

In his picture of the family washing in a cottage garden (Plate 132) Atkinson has beautifully caught the response of the village. The 'gaffer' on the gate is thoroughly experienced as a photographic prop; he knows how to look rustic. The central group of matron and children are studiously doing as they are told, earnestly *not* looking at the camera. The lady at the door, having come to see the commotion, finds herself, coy and unprepared, 'in the picture'. Or perhaps her gesture betrays guilt; as the traditional rhyme goes:

They that wash on Thursday
Are very near the last.

It was inevitable that the convention would meet abroad—Brussels first, in 1908; then Amsterdam, in 1912; and, had not untoward circumstances conspired to prevent it, France, in 1915. During the War further meetings were postponed 'until more pacific times', although there was a distinct implication that 'it would all be over by Christmas'. As the War dragged on, a concessionary meeting was called in 1918 to transact the statutory business: 'the rendezvous will probably be the zoo, because of camera restrictions elsewhere, with an evening social meeting in the city, should time, circumstances and the Food Controller permit!'[10]

Records do not say what the convention was reduced to eating that year but by then Lord Rhondda had complete control over all food and drink. It was an offence to throw rice at a wedding or to use too much starch in the laundry. The muffin man disappeared from the streets, though pets fared better: Lord Rhondda did his best to alleviate the shortage of dog biscuits, 'recognising the importance to national life of man's best friend, as Kipling termed him'.[11] The shortage of food must have hit the convention as hard as limitations on subjects or film. Had cameras been banned during the War and food remained in abundant supply, the spirit of the convention might have survived.

After the War there was a brave attempt to revive the convention's emaciated form. In 1919, at Oxford, and 1920, at Norwich, (Plates 132–6) it fed on the traditional convention diet of 'business so delightfully mixed with other things'. But the complacent swagger had gone from the 'other things'. And, more important, the actual business of photography had changed.

Inflation had, of course, taken its wartime toll. A dozen quarter-plate negatives, which, in June 1913, had cost 1s., in February 1918 cost 2s. 9d. The crucial change, however, lay elsewhere. It was perhaps in unconscious recognition of this that in 1921 the convention elected as President Mr C.H. Bothamley, who had held the same office no less than thirty-one years before. His 1921 presidential address was much too long and, at times, embarrassing but its closing words mark the end of an age:

> I feel that to the great mass of photographers the really important thing that has taken place in the last thirty years is the marked improvement, one may almost say the perfection of the manufacture of photographic materials.... As a consequence, the elementary practice of photography has become remarkably simple and certain. From one point of view this is a great gain, but I think that for many there has been a loss of that interest that arises out of difficulties and uncertainties.... The centre of interest has shifted from the processes of photography to the applications of photography. Many of the opportunities for discussion and exchange of experience that used to arise out of the less perfected processes have disappeared, and I think the difficulty of keeping up interest and enthusiasm has undoubtedly become greater.[12]

The style of Bothamley's lament is tedious and diffuse; the young in the audience, the few that there were, probably groaned at hearing an old man count the cost of technological development; but the words are oddly moving. The days of the pioneering amateurs had indeed passed and the extensive *British Journal of Photography* coverage once accorded the convention was increasingly given to the brasher usurper, the Annual Congress of the Professional Photographers' Association. 'Touch-stone' in the *Amateur Photographer* retired the 'man who worked in wet-plate days' to a harmless niche:

> The corner armchair at the club is his by long unchallenged right. He is paterfamilias and looks out upon the present situation with a shrewd and kindly eye. But in his heart of hearts he is saying that we young fellows are not really photographers. We are only the inheritors of photography. We have never undergone his own strange and fearful initiation. Paths have been made smooth for us, rough places plain, and he rather fears that we may become a boneless species because we have not wrestled through the dark, like Jacob, for a blessing.[13]

Alfred Atkinson's presidency of the convention at York in 1923 was, then, tinged with sadness. Like Bothamley and Jacob, he had wrestled in the dark. His real photographic days were recorded in albums nearly forty years old. And he was reduced in the tribute of the retiring President to 'a man keenly interested in architecture'. The hard post-war times had also reduced the convention's numbers. The photographic journals refer with regret to 'the general condition of these times' and 'unavoidable causes'. These are defensive euphemisms. Mr Bothamley spoke again in a voice from the past: 'Their society had suffered in the same way as others from the circumstances of the times but fortunately they had managed to keep together and were looking forward to a time when membership would be as big as it formerly was.'[14] Sad words; but the convention's wartime wounds were to prove lingeringly fatal.

In the official group photograph at York (Plate 137) there is hardly a man under fifty. They pose like survivors of an old campaign. There seems no place in this reunion for men who could not remember times when cameras were uncertain. The convention struggled on for another twelve years and Alfred Atkinson remained loyal to the dwindling group. The last surviving picture of his convention life is of a garden party at Steeton, Yorkshire, in 1932 (Plate 138). And as the Photographic Convention faltered, Alfred faced trouble nearer home.

FOOTNOTES OVERLEAF

[1] *British Journal of Photography*, 12 June 1896.

[2] *British Journal of Photography*, 21 July 1905.

[3] *British Journal of Photography*, 20 July 1900.

[4] *Amateur Photographer*, 4 July 1910.

[5] *Amateur Photographer*, 4 July 1905.

[6] *British Journal of Photography*, 12 July 1907.

[7] These two photographs were not taken by Alfred Atkinson but by H.M. Hastings, another member of the convention. Their coming to light was another coincidence. While writing this book, I visited some friends whom I had not seen for many years. They had a small collection of lantern slides, some of which turned out to be pictures of photographic convention excursions.

[8] *Amateur Photographer*, 31 July 1911.

[9] *British Journal of Photography*, 21 July 1899.

[10] *British Journal of Photography*, 15 February 1918.

[11] *National Food Journal*, May 1918.

[12] *British Journal of Photography*, 8 July 1921.

[13] *Amateur Photographer*, 20 March 1911.

[14] *British Journal of Photography*, 6 July 1923.

PHYLLIS ATKINSON (FRONT), CHRISTINE, KATHLEEN AND WINNIE AT HUBY, ABOUT 191

PHYLLIS (SITTING, RIGHT)
AND PLAYMATES
AT HUBY, ABOUT 1906

EVALD ('CHIPPY'),
TAIRA AND MAFELDA (LEFT THREE)
AT FILEY, ABOUT 1920

'Not yet the age of the snapshot'

CONVENTION PHOTOGRAPHERS AT MELROSE
DURING THE EDINBURGH CONVENTION, 1892;
PHOTOGRAPH BY H. M. HASTINGS

109

110 THE LEEDS CONVENTION, 1896; FROM THE RIGHT: ISAAC, POLLY AND ALFRED ATKINSON
(SITTING)

112

114

115

117

118

THE NORMAN ARCH,
ADEL CHURCH, LEEDS, 1887

'The conventioners took both pictures and tea'

PHOTOGRAPH BY H. M. HASTINGS, ABOUT 1890

120

THE CONVENTION GARDEN PARTY, ABOUT 1900

HEMINGFORD AND CAMBRIDGE, 1902

123   THE BATH CONVENTION—
EXCURSION TO BRISTOL, 1891;
PHOTOGRAPH BY H. M. HASTINGS

124   THE BATH CONVENTION—
EXCURSION TO GLASTONBURY, 1891;
PHOTOGRAPH BY H. M. HASTINGS

6

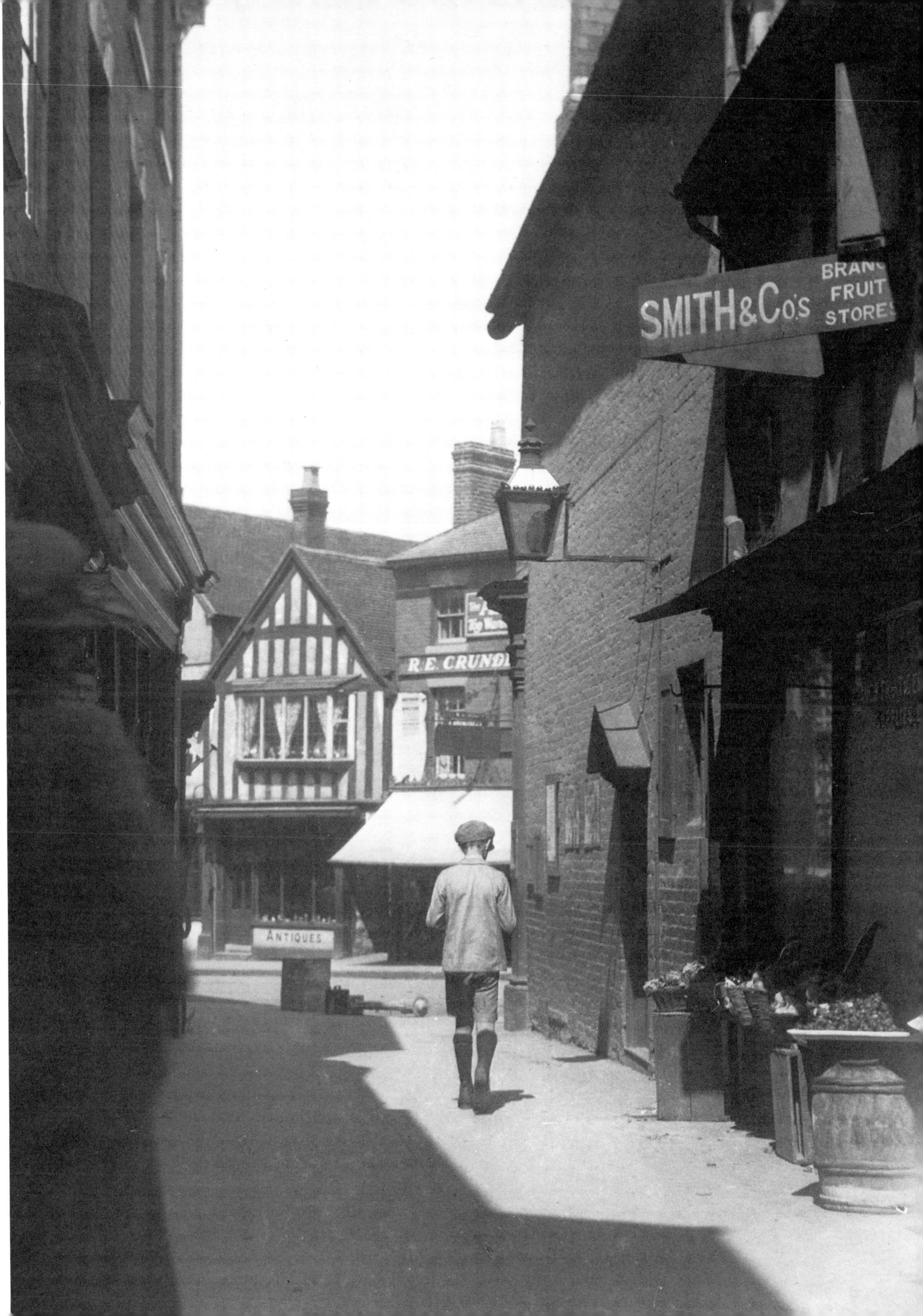

127 and 128
THE GLOUCESTER CONVENTION, 1899;
CHEDDAR GORGE AND A
BORDER CASTLE

132 to 136
THE CONVENTION AT
NORWICH, 1920

137 ALFRED ATKINSON AS PRESIDENT OF THE CONVENTION AT YORK, 1923

138 THE CONVENTION AT ILKLEY, 1932

DIMINUENDO

WHAT I LEARNED of the Atkinsons' leisure showed that from the turn of the century it was 'Summer, in some ways, always'.[1] For twenty years at least the Atkinsons stretched the 'long week-end' until it almost squeezed out the week. With such dazzling evidence of time on their hands and money to be spent, I assumed that the family building business was booming and, for much of the time, had to take care of itself. Indeed, there was solid proof of the boom in the city of Leeds. In the first twenty years of this century H. Atkinson and Sons Ltd won huge municipal contracts for the City of Leeds Training College in Beckett's Park, the Ministry of Pensions Hospital at Chapeltown and Lawnswood Crematorium. In at least one part of his welfare—in his schooling, his ill-health or at his end—the average citizen of Leeds might well benefit from the Victorian enterprise of Henry Atkinson. He and his sons might well have adopted Christopher Wren's memorial plaque for themselves: 'If you would see his memorial, then look around you'.

After 1912 Alfred Atkinson was in sole control of the firm; his elder brother and partner, Isaac, died at the early age of forty-nine. The few available pictures of men at work during this time suggest an army such as Henry Atkinson never dreamed of. Fortunately, two account books survive from these lush pastures before 1920. They were found, mildewed with damp, on the floor of the garage at Huby after the dealers had taken the pickings. Solid, leather-bound tomes, beautifully kept by a clerk in an immaculate hand, they exude security. During the First World War 'Business as usual', as the current boast went, would have been an understatement. *The Times*, in a series, 'England in Time of War', published from December 1914 to February 1915, drew this laudatory picture of Leeds: 'Men and women are toiling all day long into the night and some of them are making small fortunes. Indeed,

the city has probably never been so prosperous.'

Alfred Atkinson's wages bill topped £900 per week. How many hands, I wondered, did that represent. The government's 'Earning and Hours Inquiry Report' (of 1910) had some helpful figures: the one million employees in the building trades were paid a rate of between 7d. and 9d. per hour for an average 45-hour winter week and 52 hours in the summer. Average earnings in a full summer week in Yorkshire in 1906 were quoted at 33s. 1d. With a weekly wages bill of over £900, even allowing for a few years' inflation, Alfred Atkinson must at times have been paying over 400 men.

One man, at least, who had served Henry Atkinson and Sons Ltd, had memories of his boyhood revived by reading of my researches.

Raymond Hull had now retired to Knaresborough where he tended an immaculate garden and composed rhymes for his grandchildren. He talked of his 'deep respect for a grand old firm'. His father, James Hull, first entered the firm when his son was just a baby at the time of the building of the Training College in Beckett's Park. James Hull was timekeeper on the site. His wife wheeled her son in the pram from nearby Kirkstall most days to deliver James's sandwiches fresh from the kitchen. On the site the infant Raymond toured the work in the arms of Percy Massey, then an office boy but later to become Foreman Joiner. Twelve years later, in 1924, Raymond began his apprenticeship. He spent his first working days under his father's nose at Knostrop Sewage Works before moving to a more salubrious setting in the workshop in Carlton Hill (Plate 139) as joiner's apprentice on 12s. 11d. per week.

Even the menial tasks, however, could be fraught with adventure. Once, as tea boy, Raymond eked out the hot water by dipping into the pan in which all the glue-pots stood. In those days, too, the cumbersome and unsprung handcart was standard transport for collecting and delivering building materials around the hilly and cobbled neighbourhood of Woodhouse Lane (in the Carlton Hill district). With a heavy load of bricks, cement and 'sundries', it could be too much for a young apprentice to control. Raymond remembered sprawling headlong in Portland Street *en route* to the Nurses' Home site in Calverley Street, having hit a pothole and anticipated the unloading. On another occasion he fought a grim battle with the wind while carrying a huge sheet of plywood from Ilingworth, Ingham and Co. in Black Bull Street. But for the help of a sympathetic pedestrian, the boy and his load would have been whisked off the exposed Crown Point Bridge into the River Aire beneath. The Saturday morning task was to paste up outside the premises in Carlton Hill details of the following week's films at the Cottage Road cinema. The Atkinson firm had shares in the place, having refurbished its interior. It was there, sporting his new 'plusses', Raymond took his wife on their first date. He knew the best courting seats, having installed them himself.

Raymond Hull remembered the passing of the firm's horse and cart in the care of George Rhodes who lived at the Vicarage, near Headingley Station. The new, more efficient workhorses were three lorries: one 'Vulcan', one 'Peerless' and one 'A.E.C.'.

Raymond could not say much about 'Mr Alfred' himself, though he remembered the dapper figure in pin-stripe trousers and smart, black jacket. Mr Alfred was, apparently, not around the works very much, only a few hours at a time, 'just to keep his eye in'.

I found only four documents to tell the remaining story of the family firm. They are like an author's conflicting drafts of how he wished the event. One — a beautifully illustrated certificate of Alfred Atkinson's presidency of the Yorkshire Builders' Federation in 1935 — fittingly ends the fairy tale of the young artisan who walked off the country estate to seek fortune in the city; the pauper becomes prince.

The other three documents, however, chronicle a more medieval tale where prosperity is counted too soon before the wheel turns. Business at H. Atkinson and Sons was already on the slippery slope when Alfred's brother, Henry George, apprehensive of his capital in the business, wrote, on 4 September 1933: '... I hope you will have a clear, well-digested and effective scheme to put before us on Thursday so that matters may be licked into shape without waste of time.' Whatever the plan was, it placated Henry George for a while but Alfred's continuing indulgent lifestyle becomes, in the circumstances, a sad flourish. A year later, in August 1934, Henry George wrote again, this time with scarcely muted asperity: 'The conditions on which the firm was allowed to continue business have not been adhered to.... The executors feel that you are not treating the matter with that seriousness it demands and must ask you to have the matter dealt with at once. Don't let us have any unpleasantness over the matter.'

The last page in this account of the harsher denouement is the liquidator's statement, dated 1937. Preferential shareholders saved their capital but ordinary shareholders were compensated at only a halfpenny per share.

The reasons for this collapse one can only infer. The national building boom one might have expected after the First World War seems to have been slow, even though the shortage of houses was acute (a 1921 census shows three-quarters of a million more families than 'separate dwellings'). Materials were scarce and costly and the skilled labour force had been halved in four years when no apprentices were recruited. The Director General for Housing, appointed in 1919, offered subsidies but only enough to ripple the market's stagnant surface. In the 1920s things looked up, however. Government grants and cheaper material led to a building boom which was a steadying factor in the life of a nation on the downward run of a trade depression. At the time, in 1923 and 1924, Alfred Atkinson's men were building up-market villas on the Otley Old Road and in Headingley. Subsidies continued throughout the decade until the fall of the Labour Government in 1931 and the Coalition's implementing the cuts proposed in the May Report — including an end of aid to housebuilding. From 1932 the growth in housebuilding was financed largely by the building societies; the new government subsidies from 1935 were really designed to encourage slum clearance.

Somewhere among this financial uncertainty Alfred Atkinson's business finally foundered, although the currents that disturbed its prosperous voyage surfaced long before. Sidney Webb's famous Clause Four for the Labour Party's Constitution (1918) envisaged a force which should shake the foundations of Fir Tree House; he aimed 'to secure for the producers by hand or by brain the full fruits of their industry and the most equitable distribution thereof that may be possible, upon the basis of common ownership of the means of production and the best obtainable system of popular administration and the control of each industry or service.' Alfred Atkinson was never a Union man; he thought his men were better off without one.

Some suggest that Alfred himself was to blame for the firm's decline. They say that, after old Henry's death, Isaac had the acumen where Alfred had only style. When Isaac died before the completion of the Training College, Arthur Ashley, as manager, took over the helm. Some of the Atkinson family did not like him; they found him 'too big for his boots'. They say he even had the cheek to talk to others of 'his' firm. Fred Whitaker, Alfred's nephew, also worked in the business but he resigned after the War, embittered at not getting a seat on the Board; he became a highly successful civil engineer. When Ashley left, too, Alfred had to face the harsh light of business and found it too glaring. The firm lost its impetus and came to a halt. There were rumours of a takeover but Alfred refused to sell the family name, believing that most other builders threw up their buildings in slapdash fashion and would not preserve the standards for which the Atkinsons were known.

There is an appealing superstition, popular among the Elizabethans, which sees a link between national and domestic disasters. The year 1936 was ominously unsettled at both levels. As the Atkinsons' family business, a monument to the enterprise of an earlier time, collapsed round their ears, the Crystal Palace,[2] that great Palladium of Victorianism, also came down in flames. Henry Atkinson, Alfred's father, had visited the Crystal Palace in the year of its opening and the Great Exhibition there would have fired his ambition to found his own business. The huge arches of the Crystal Palace, therefore,

effectively span the history of H. Atkinson and Sons. In the same year which saw the end of them both, Polly Atkinson died, two days before the abdication of the King.

On 31 December 1936 the *Daily Telegraph* paid tribute to the year:

Certain years in history seem to have been desperately charged with fate. Of their number is the year whose last hours are now passing. It is not that 1936 will be memorable by the magnitude of its actual disasters. But it has abounded in events which have seemed to bring catastrophe near.

Alfred Atkinson survived his wife by nine years. He died on 6 January 1945.

Kathleen, Alfred's unmarried daughter, lived on alone for another thirty years at Fir Tree House. It is easy, and some have done it, to sentimentalise the picture. But thirty years is half a lifetime and Kathleen had reason to be both lonely and envious. Idolised by her parents, she had not had much social success. Her contemporaries remember her as always 'a little odd', even as a girl. Her sister married and set up home elsewhere; Kathleen's love for her cousin was not returned and she found no one else. Her only male company, apart from her father, was Battinson, the chauffeur. He would take her for drives and she helped on the car. She also had painting lessons in Pannal from a Mr Smith but there was nothing Bohemian in that.

After the death of her parents, Kathleen's life must have been bleak, despite the friends who came to see her. There is no surprise—but no compensation either—that in her last fifteen years she lived increasingly for the past. Even that animation was suspended in her father's photographs and lantern slides shut away in cupboards. As time passed, she stood still and eventually turned back, recreating for herself the rituals of her childhood. If a neighbour cooked her a meal, Kathleen might lay the table with the family silver for her parents and sister. If she incurred any expenses, it was always with the confidence that 'Daddy will pay'. Kathleen lived in the world of her father's photographs, where his esteem still promised a bright future. Miss-Havisham-like, she left things untouched and, when she died, in January 1975, the house had become both a museum and a sad memorial to an unfulfilled life.

Two months after Kathleen's death, the contents of the house came under the hammer. Personal possessions became collectors' items and were scattered in search of high prices. The children's toys, their dolls and their play costumes, were displayed for an audience less concerned with entertainment but who were pleased none the less. A carpet runner, which for years had served to catch grease in front of the cooker, fetched a thousand pounds. Alfred's cameras and plates were exposed again. The brass and mahogany gear—'Lot 47, Pearson and Denham, full-plate camera; Lot 49, Carbide-gas Lantern-slide projector'—advertised its worth and was eagerly snapped up. But the negatives and slides were less prized. They passed through unappreciative, though careful, hands to arrive intact on a market stall in Wakefield.

In the month that I bought the negatives, August 1975, the house and errant garden were sold by auction into the speculative market. Within months the new owner had made a quick profit by reselling the house and dividing most of the garden into building lots. Three luxury houses now stand on the overgrown remains. Carlton Hill, the original site of the Atkinsons' business and home, has also gone. It made way for a new dual-carriageway traffic complex through Leeds city centre. In a different way, perhaps, from Henry Atkinson's time, this 'Motorway City of the North' is still anxious to go places.

Even the family graves have been disturbed. Graves number 13429 (Hebden) and 10420 (Atkinson) now lie buried only in computerised records on the shelves of Leeds Local History Library. The bones themselves lay under what is now the Henry Price Building on Leeds University campus.

Alfred and Polly Atkinson, however, have escaped. They lie, uneasily, in the graveyard at Weeton church, oddly out of place, Congregationalists in an Anglican setting.

[1] Laurie Lee, *Cider with Rosie.*
[2] There is a final link here with Leeds Town Hall. Joseph Paxton, who conceived the audacious glasshouse in London's Hyde Park, was consulted by the Town Council committee about the building of the new Town Hall.

7

CODA

THE STORY OF Alfred Atkinson's photographs, which opened humbly on a junk stall with a boxful of glass and a phrase of two words, caught up others as well as myself. In the spring of 1976, eight months after I had bought the negatives, I wrote to BBC North, hoping the television coverage, even on a small scale, might put me in touch with others who knew the Atkinsons at Huby. Besides, the project was, in the best sense, regional and popular. In the end the BBC made a film of two stories in one— family saga and detective yarn. Making the film brought a more detached view of the thing as a whole.

The Atkinson family story has an organic shape of growth and decay. It is in a double sense the story of a 'house' in which the stones at Huby and Carlton Hill can speak for the people. The Carlton Hill terrace, built to satisfy primary needs, served more body than soul. Here Henry Atkinson was, in Dr Smiles' phrase, 'yoked to the car of toil'—at least, in the early years. The family's transition thereafter from workhorse to passenger is echoed in the mixed structure of Fir Tree House, part cottage, part manor. Alfred Atkinson's extensions there at the turn of this century gave space for comfort without the style that belongs to architecture, not mere building.

Nevertheless, the Atkinsons loved Fir Tree House and would have hoped that, in an appropriate phrase of John Ruskin's, the 'Lamp of Memory' would burn brightly there. We may cringe at his rhetoric and coolly accept that houses live and die, but Ruskin says what many affluent Victorians felt for their homes in the way that they felt it:

There is sanctity in a good man's house which cannot be renewed in every tenement that rises on its ruins: and I believe that good men would generally feel that, having spent their lives

happily and honourably, they would be grieved, at the close of them, to think that their earthly abode, which had seen, and seemed almost to sympathise with all their honour, their gladness or their suffering—that this, with all the record it bore of them, and all material things that they loved and ruled over, and set the stamp of themselves upon—was to be swept away ... that though there was a monument in the church, there was no monument in the hearth and house to them; that ... the places that had sheltered and comforted them were dragged down to the dust.[1]

Although the demolition gangs put out the light at Carlton Hill and new houses stand in the grounds at Huby, Fir Tree House is in hands sensitive to the touch of its history and anxious to preserve it. In their preliminary work the new owners, Martin and Janet Owen, have already added flesh to the story. Despite the rapacious dealers, who even tore light fittings from the ceilings, the house had some secrets left. In clearing out the garage, Martin opened cupboards that had been kept shut for years. In one he found the clean, white skeleton of a cat, curled up on a shelf like a forgotten toy. In another cupboard were rolls of linen-backed paper, some nibbled by mice. They were sets of plans, beautifully drawn and then coloured by hand, for the houses built by H. Atkinson and Sons from the 1860s, and also details of the extension at Fir Tree House after 1904.

There is a memorial, too, much more eloquent than stones, in the photographs and lantern slides. Publicity has made them public property and inevitably led to an exhibition, which helped me stand back from the pictures. Planning the exhibition was a challenge. As a casual visitor to galleries, I had no more idea of what was involved than most of a theatre audience knows or cares about the world in the wings. If the analogy holds, producing plays should have told me there were problems ahead and that one needed the faith that it would be 'all right on the night'.

The selection of prints inevitably reflected our interests, even at the expense of the photographer's. Atkinson, as a professional builder, gave more than a glance at the buildings he passed and his interest in stone was more than artisan. He had an historical sense and discerning taste. However, his competent studies of ubiquitous pillars and vaulting (Plates 140 and 141) are those we first discarded in compiling the exhibition. In some of these pictures, at least, the rigours of stone are somewhat softened by carefully placed figures (Plates 142 and 143).

Atkinson's negatives were so well preserved that hardly any of the prints in the exhibition or this book needed retouching. Some of the more intractable negatives needed 'burning-in' or 'holding-back', where, in the picture, spillage of light through window or leaves caused an ugly glare or where clouds in the sky needed careful cajoling. One of the best pictures, in fact, gave the most trouble (Plate 81). To take a picture at all in such adverse conditions was bold; even a modern, coated lens could hardly deal with the contrast of dim shadows and glaring daylight from the windows. The trickiest feature was the light flaring from the white dresses and windows and over-exposing the surrounding areas.[2]

Advertising put out before the exhibition talked of Alfred Atkinson's 'humble, enquiring and often beautiful vision'. That was embarrassingly pretentious. 'Vision', though a cliché of criticism, has the wrong feel in this context. It makes a pompous claim which is at odds with the purpose of the photographs. However, in a quite ordinary sense, Alfred Atkinson had his way of looking—or, more passively, his way of seeing—even though it may have been typical of a class and an age. What internal links, then, hold the pictures together?

One link between the pictures is easily confused with an aura they have for us from being seen at a distance, through a veil of time. The screen we look through is our own nostalgia for small boats, rustic cottages and old-fashioned clothes. However, quite apart from our repining, there is an ethos in Alfred Atkinson's choice of subjects. In his pictures there

are no shops, no factories and only streets that are picturesque. That limitation is crucial. When photographers like Atkinson stood with their backs to the city when they looked through the viewfinder (Plates 144 and 145), they were demonstrating that their photography had nothing to do with the crushing and squalid routines of industrial life. Photographic albums and lantern-slide shows were to them vivid reminders that the grass which grew elsewhere was still literally greener. And that, after all, is what most casual snapshots do today, taken at weekends or on holidays when work is not master. If Alfred Atkinson's photographs strike people today as 'Romantic'—and many have said just that—it is not because, in the semi-technical meaning of the word, he consciously valued heart before head; nor because the pictures are evocatively ancient. They are, frankly, escapist.

The exhibition offered the photographs primarily as images and many will stand independently, not shored up by biography. Still pictures alone, however, do not tell a story which has come alive. Alfred Atkinson's photographs are more than an hitherto unknown photographer's 'work'. They are a record of his family and friends (Plate 146). There is a conflict here, inherent in photography, between two ways of creating a picture. In the first, the picture is a slow, deliberate and self-contained artefact in which the artist chooses his point of view and then orders his subject, restraining Nature by Art, as eighteenth-century critics would have said. This school of photography takes its canons from traditional painting. Early photographers did, in fact, ape the two great genres of oil-painting: landscapes and portraits. The cumbersome early cameras and slow processes of photography would have encouraged them to think like artists with easels. Painters and photographers worked interdependently, despite the understandable rivalry between them, jealously guarding their domains. Painters used photographs for models and sought (especially the Pre-Raphaelites, much supported by John Ruskin before the 1860s) 'the correct representation of real things'. In return, photographers tried to achieve a painter's freedom from merely recording what was there.

In some of his photographs Alfred Atkinson 'painted' his picture and in these more deliberate studies, the subjects have, as it were, no life outside.

People are reduced to carefully-placed objects, unnaturally perched on benches or in boats (Plates 89, 147 and 148). They look into the picture and away from the camera, as if to deny any relationship with the photographer. The world is excluded, and that means us. Nothing in these pictures reaches outside: they are introspective. Even fragments of path seem complete; where they go round the corner does not matter.

Photographic subjects, however, will not always obey rules. In some of Alfred Atkinson's more deliberate pictures there is wilful but touching disobedience on the part of the subjects. In the village square (Plate 149) a little girl detaches herself from the organised human interest to create a diversion of her own, playing hide-and-seek round the corner. In the picture of the cottage garden at Tintern (Plate 131) a woman unexpectedly comes to the door; her response is a mute but loud comment on the fixing of the others.

In one picture (Plate 1) the contrast is symbolic. In a farmyard two fashionable drawing-room ornaments in bustles and boaters pretend to be feeding the chickens. There are other genteel appendages: the tame dog at their feet, and the dairymaid and the groom in their respectable uniforms, all carefully placed to illustrate 'Life on the Farm'. But the life in the picture, like the real life on the farm, goes on elsewhere and ignores the photographer. The blurred chickens scurry round and, in the background, a true worker (in his braces) has shambled into the edge of the frame. In the end the photograph, despite Atkinson perhaps, captures two quite different ways of seeing. The contrast between them is central to Victorian life, in which the proper and the animal could never be reconciled.

These details in which Atkinson caught life 'as it is' rather than saying cheese for the camera, are part of a second way of creating pictures, more as windows on the the world. This is a function of instantaneous photography. By 1858 camera speeds of one fiftieth of a second were possible and allowed photographers to freeze 'the still point of the turning world':

Walking figures, running figures, falling figures, equestrian figures and vehicles, all caught in their acts without the slightest appearance of movement or imperfect definition. Here is a lad transfixed in the act of falling, flying forward, as something has tripped him up; he remains on the slide doomed neither to fall farther nor rise again.[3]

However, the fact of sharpness and the convention of the snapshot (the artless distribution of figures and the cutting off of objects at the edge of the pictures)—these are less important in themselves than what they imply about the connection between the pictures and the world outside. In snapshots the external world is always implied; we continually recognise that a person's entrance into the picture is an exit from somewhere else, and vice versa. Snapshots assert that we continue to live even when we are stopped in a picture; and that we live as much, if not more, through our relationships outside the picture than within the truncated image.

In that sense, all the words in this book—the history of the Atkinson family and meetings with old people who were young in the photographs—are not merely background but part of the substance of the pictures. Snapshots reach out not just to the physical world outside the picture; they also look backwards and forwards in time. We ask of people in photographs how they came to be there or what they did with their lives.

One of Alfred Atkinson's photographs is particularly laden with echoes through time (Plate 150). Kathleen Atkinson, her sister and her friends masquerade in the garden in fancy dress to celebrate Kathleen's twenty-first birthday. Their costumes unite the girls in a sense of celebration but also, in their peculiarity, they point to future, separate lives. Kathleen Atkinson (bottom left), her sister, Christine (the clown), and Alice Armitage (the gypsy) I had followed from their sunny childhood to the confusion, restraints or decline of old age. Two of the remaining girls, Mary Heath and Madeleine Taite—the 'Bung Girls' they were called—whiled away weekends at a bungalow in Huby. The last girl, Muriel Hoyte (the geisha), may have lived a more conventional life than her costume suggests but her past and present are rich none the less.

When I met Miss Hoyte, I realised that her Japanese robes in the fancy dress picture were apt: she considered herself a foreigner at Huby. 'Imposter' is actually the word she chose, having been born in London and only moving to Huby, via Liverpool, during the First World War. Her life in the village for over sixty years since then—for twenty of them as schoolmistress by popular demand—had made her, though she denied it, a central figure.

Her house was next door but one to Fir Tree House, though it was not easy to trace her. Her front gate, the victim at once of disuse and road improvements, was nailed up and overgrown with cotoneaster and ivy, while the drive she shared with her neighbour wound round to a bewildering ensemble of doors. Miss Hoyte's house had once been two and had never shaken off its dual personality. I found Miss Hoyte—or, rather, she found me—in the garden. She led me into the office after carefully negotiating the full-length screen at the front door that deterred any trespassing cats. 'Come into the office' was an echo of the days when the house was a school but it also showed the businesslike way in which Miss Hoyte still ran her life.

She was a lady of quite overwhelming energy, with little patience for those of her sex educated only, as she said, in the three C's—children, cooking and clothes. In her own time she had known men defer to her knowledge of fishing. She was worried that she might not cram into her life all that she wanted to do, including a search into her own remarkable family. Her great-grandfather on one side was Lord Mayor of Dublin. His enormous portrait loomed over the stairs at Huby and still bore the scars where Sinn Feiners hacked it with a knife to demonstrate their republican zeal. On the other side of the family, Miss Hoyte's great-grandmother was the daughter of Thomas Hazlehurst, painter of miniatures. She married a wastrel who gambled them into ruin. Then she made her own way as a nurse in London, recording the details of her cases almost as narratives. The Earl of Ripon, whom she tended in 1856, consigned her, she claimed, to a shameful garret at the top of the house on a cold, wet day, with no fire, no counterpane, no pillow, only two thin calico sheets and a mildewed glass that hardly gave back her reflection.

Though her forebears occupied some of her time, Miss Hoyte's own life, too, positively sparkled. Her work in Huby village school spanned two generations in which her later, wartime charges were the children of her earlier pupils. She talked of them all as her relatives, not clients. The younger ones were her 'grandchildren' and she treated photographs as a family album, tracing likenesses. Her teaching philosophy must have been refreshingly free from dogma. She culled from Froebel, Montessori and the rest what she thought worthwhile but, in the end, remained simply herself, teaching a dozen or more lessons in a single room.

Miss Hoyte was, at first, one face out of six in a picture; meeting her along with the others made that flimsy pictorial coincidence only a nexus of divergent lives.

People in snapshots, then, belong in the picture and elsewhere. In one seaside picture (Plate 151) the donkey man is crudely bisected. The half that we see is an awkward instrusion into a family holiday moment that in the future will be cherished by parents and seen as a source of embarrassment by their growing children. The donkeyman's other foot is planted in a different world, where ex-fishermen are reduced to scratching a living by selling diversion to children.

Sometimes people metaphorically, if not literally, look out of the picture. They disappear round mysterious corners (Plate 53) or look over walls (Plate 112) and thereby extend the picture beyond the borders of the prints. The men who stare out to sea, of course, do belong in the picture; their poses say they have time on their hands, both the working men and the more affluent holiday-maker on the left peering through glasses. His daughter (?), bored, perhaps by the sameness of the waves, turns away and prods the pavement with her father's walking-stick. She is anxious to be off, like the dog, which stares so intently at something out of frame it can only be accident that delays him long enough to be photographed. The cat in Kathleen Atkinson's grasp (Plate 152) is poised even more precariously. So, too, in a sense are the people at the picnic (Plate 79). They have agreed to be photographed and have grouped themselves. Some have switched on the right look, especially the man at the back in the bowler and with his pipe. But, rather than wait for all the poses, Atkinson anticipated them—perhaps the shutter simply 'went off' too early. The result is a photograph of people waiting to be photographed and that has much more life than any formal portrait.

The two theoretical ideals, snapshots and studies, are really ends of a continuum. Those who stood intractably at one pole or the other during the great Victorian debates on photography as 'Art' missed the singular richness of powerful pictures which can seem both spontaneously caught and pictorially 'right'. Alfred Atkinson's photograph of Whitby fisherfolk at work on a new catch in their cobles (Plate 33) seems just such a picture. There are relaxed patterns in the misaligned boats and the repeated clutter of fish, baskets and tackle in each. The perspective, which is, after all, only an accident of the tide, brings us unobserved close into the work going on. A fisherman steps up out of the picture towards us; his movement is central and his seaboot is, appropriately, the only blur in the picture. This photograph contrasts with another, taken at the same time, of boats bobbing too neatly on their reflections (Plate 32). For all their beauty, they have the idleness of painted ships on painted oceans.

Such formal analysis can destroy the pictures; it may reduce them to cleverly-made things by translating our feelings for images of real life into disinterested terms. We may be struck by Alfred Atkinson's sense of a 'good picture' but the real emotional charge of his photographs probably lies elsewhere. Our response to them includes our feelings for the man and his world—our nostalgia or embarrassment for an age of blithe optimism which believed in the ultimate perfectability of things, an age in which slums and grubby children, if they were photographed at all, were usually seen as picturesque vestiges which the march of man and machines would soon sweep away (Plate 153). And if, recognising this, we still feel nostalgia for Alfred Atkinson's pictures, perhaps that is only to say that we still secretly cling to the same comforting illusion.

[1] J. Ruskin *The Seven Lamps of Architecture*, 1849.

[2] This effect of 'halation' occurs when the light penetrating the emulsion in light areas of the picture is refracted during exposure in the camera back from the uncoated side of the glass through the emulsion to erode darker areas. Sometimes it can be an annoying distraction but, occasionally, when it softens the outline of foliage against the sky, it lends an 'Impressionist' feel—as in the later landscapes of Corot. Contemporary critics did not all like the effect—'They are not trees; they are smoke'.

[3] *Photo News*, 8 October 1861.

139

'Competent studies of ubiquitous pillars and vaulting'

140

GLOUCESTER CATHEDRAL CLOISTERS
AND SCRIPTORIUM, 1899

141

ST CUTHBERT'S FONT, FISHLAKE, 1890

'The rigours of stone softened by carefully-placed figures'

142   RAGLAN CASTLE, 1899
143   HARDWICK HALL, 1895

143

144   145

'The grass which grew elsewhere was still literally greener' 1890

147

'*Unnaturally perched on benches*' 1895 AND 1910

148

149

A VILLAGE SQUARE, ABOUT 1890

KATHLEEN ATKINSON'S TWENTY-FIRST
BIRTHDAY PARTY, 1920

152

KATHLEEN ATKINSON,
ABOUT 1905

'Picturesque vestiges' ABOUT 1890

Appendix:
The Arlington Fiasco

AS HIS FAMILY business began to creak and show signs of strain, Alfred Atkinson ventured on a hugely ambitious scheme elsewhere which promised vast returns but became a nightmare of mounting expense and despair. The history of this 'miserable project' (as it was later referred to) can be pieced together from a voluminous file of hundreds of items of correspondence which survives in the hands of Godfrey Linfoot. It is a story of those who thought they had the Midas touch seeing the glister turn to dust. Writing the correspondence alone would occupy a small lifetime running from the ingenuousness of youth to an embittered old age

In 1930 'four gentlemen' formed a syndicate to buy and develop the old Arlington Hotel, Brighton, facing the Marine Parade, near the Aquarium and next to the South Down Motor Coach Station. Alfred Atkinson had three partners—Mr M., a Scottish lawyer (who was later to regret that 'the law is better in Scotland than it is in England'); Mr K., managing director of a London hotel; and Mr L., also in the hotel business and 'in close touch with various financial interests'. The four were optimistic: as a draft prospectus claimed—'Hotel enterprises represent incontestably a fecund source of fortunate and remunerative investment'. They envisaged a hotel and restaurant which at peak times would cater for nearly a thousand people. To that end they proposed setting up a public company with capital of over a quarter of a million pounds sterling, the money to be raised through a London-based trust with a banking organisation and stockbroker in Brussels. The Belgian financiers received £1,250 advance commission. From October 1931, with contracts signed and plans approved, the syndicate had only to wait. Thereafter, however, everything went wrong and disasters piled up.

The syndicate found themselves victims of what they described as a 'fraudulent gang' of 'arch scoundrels' which made confident promises, pocketed advances and then did nothing. When it became clear that none of the promised capital would come from across the channel, the syndicate embarked on the long, costly and vain struggle to recover their money. The Belgians prevaricated: they had a (farcical) independent report on the syndicate's plans by a Frenchman who, with no knowledge of English property prices, valued the existing hotel at twenty-five per cent of the purchase price and, with no knowledge of English building costs, said a new hotel could be built on the continent for half the estimate.

Meanwhile, a bank reference reported ominously on the Belgian company and, worse, two journals, *Truth* (October 1933) and *John Bull* (January 1933) blew the gaff on the international swindle which several well-intentioned but naïve British businessmen had fallen foul of. Then a Brussels newspaper reported that the co-directors of the Belgian firm, the Brothers Gavinet of French extraction, had been extradited to Paris, having offered capital in France to the crazy extent of 2,000,000,000 francs. Since the Brothers Gavinet now languished in La Santé prison and their premises in Brussels had been seized by a mortgage company, the syndicate turned on the Belgian stockbroker; but their case was hopelessly weakened by the mistranslation of one, apparently innocent word in the French version of the original contract ('an arbiter' rendered as 'des arbitres'). When their correspondence expired in September 1934, Alfred Atkinson and Mr M., the most tenacious of the syndicate, were debating whether to cut their losses or set up a long search for fellow victims in the hope of interesting the Director of Public Prosecutions. Although they had long run out of patience, Alfred and Mr M. disliked the thought of 'those swindlers getting off with their plunder'.

There were pressing problems, too, in England. The architect had been demanding fees for work which the syndicate denied authorising and the London solicitors' costs had been mounting unpaid for three years. When the 23-page bill was finally submitted, one of the syndicate, Mr L., had died, leaving only 'very Large debts'—to Mr M., to a waiter at his hotel and to an old lady who could ill afford the loss of £300. It also emerged that Mr L. stood to gain £12,000 secret commission on the purchase of the Arlington and had been negotiating with the Belgians on his own. Mr K. now had very cold feet; he wanted no more trouble or expense and refused to recognise outstanding debts.

This disastrous network of shady dealing, ill-feeling and anxiety may account for what Henry George Atkinson saw as his brother Alfred's 'dilatoriness' in facing the increasing problems of the family business in Leeds. Who would notice a minnow on one hook if there were a shark on the other? In the circumstances, the sunny diversions which fill the pages of Polly Atkinson's diaries must have been a blessing.

Select Bibliography

For social history
Bailey, Leslie. *Scrapbook 1900–14* (Frederick Muller, London, 1957)
Beeton, Mrs Isabel. *The Book of Household Management* (Jonathan Cape, London, 1961; originally published by S.L. Beeton, 1861)
Briggs, Asa. *Victorian People* (Penguin, London, 1965)
—*Victorian Cities* (Penguin, London, 1968)
Connington, C. Willett. *English Clothing in the Nineteenth Century* (Faber, London, 1937)
Graves, Robert and Hodge, Alan. *The Long Weekend: A Social History of Great Britain, 1918–39* (Faber, London, 1940)
Harrison, Brian. *Drink and the Victorians* (Faber, London, 1971)
Hodge, Alan and Graves, Robert. *The Long Weekend: A Social History of Great Britain, 1918–39* (Faber, London, 1940)

Keating, Peter, ed. *Into Unknown England, 1886–1913* (Fontana, London, 1976)
Laver, James. *Edwardian Promenade* (Edward Hulton, London, 1958)
Peel, The Hon. Mrs C. C. *Life's Enchanted Cup* (John Lane, London, 1933)
Pike, E. Royston. *Human Documents of the Age of the Forsytes* (Allen & Unwin, London, 1969)
—*Human Documents of the Lloyd George Era* (Allen & Unwin, London, 1972)
Thompson, Brian. *A Portrait of Leeds* (Robert Hale, London, 1971)
Wood, Sydney. *Britain's Inter-War Years* (Blackie, Glasgow, 1975)

For history of travel
Black's Picturesque Guide to Yorkshire (Adam & Charles Black, Edinburgh, 1864)
Hern, Anthony. *The Seaside Holiday: A History of the English Seaside Resort* (Cresset Press, London, 1967)
Nicholson, Norman. *The Lakers* (Robert Hale, London, 1955)
Plimlott, J. A. R. *The Englishman's Holiday* (Faber, London, 1947)
Sanders, Ruth Manning. *Seaside England* (Batsford, London, 1951)
Simmons, Jack, ed. *A Devon Anthology* (Macmillan, London, 1971)
Swinglehurst, Edmund. *The Romantic Journey: The Story of Thomas Cook and Victorian Travel* (Pica Editions, London, 1974)

For history of photography
Berger, John. *Ways of Seeing* (B.B.C and Penguin, London, 1972)
Gernsheim, Helmut. *A Concise History of Photography* (Thames & Hudson, London, 1965)
Greenhill, Basil. *A Victorian Maritime Album* (Patrick Stephens, Cambridge, 1974)
Hiley, Michael. *Frank Sutcliffe: Photographer of Whitby* (Gordon Fraser, London, 1974)
Scharf, Aaron. *Art and Photography* (Penguin, London, 1974)
The Amateur Photographer (1880–1920)
The British Journal of Photography (1880–1920)

A Family Tree

HENRY ATKINSON = Ellen Backhouse
1823-1892   1827-1908

Fred Whitaker = Annie Backhouse

→ Whitaker family

HENRY = Annie Elizabeth Nichols
GEORGE
1857-1953

ISAAC = Maud Mary Carr
1863-1912

Kate = Edward Brook

→ Brook family

Mary Ellen = George Rogers Carr

→ Carr Family

Iris Ellen   PHYLLIS MAUD
b. 1902

Margaret Winifred   Henry

Margherita Ursula Wolfe = Edgar David   Henry Nichols

Gertude = Alvin Mahoney

→ Mahoney family

Christine Ellen = Herbert Dove

WILLIAM HEBDEN = Ann Goulds
d. 1904

ALFRED WILLIAM ATKINSON
1864-1945

Norman Edward   Arthur

WILLIAM
THOMAS HEBDEN
1868-1888

MARY ('POLLY') HEBDEN =
1865-1936

Ethel Hebden Atkinson
d. 1897 aged 2 months

KATHLEEN IRENE ATKINSON
1899-1975

Ruth Consola Elizabeth

CHRISTINE ATKINSON = Dr Ernest Linfoot
b. 1902

Janet M. Tyrrell = GODFREY ATKINSON LINFOOT
b. 1930

→

Dorothy Joan
Penrice (2) = John David = (1) Barbara Joyce Middlebrook

JONATHAN GEORGE = Isobel Lindsay
b. 1943   Anderson

→

Georgina Lucy = Peter Eugene
Watson

Jason Christopher = Elsie Hancock

→